The Beginner's Guide to
Edible Herbs

The mission of Storey Publishing is to serve our customers by publishing practical information that encourages personal independence in harmony with the environment.

Edited by Carleen Madigan and Sarah Guare
Art direction and book design by Alethea Morrison
Text production by Liseann Karandisecky

Photography by © Saxon Holt

Additional editorial assistance by Andrea Chesman
Indexed by Eileen Clawson

Storey Publishing
210 MASS MoCA Way
North Adams, MA 01247
www.storey.com

Printed in Canada by Transcontinental Printing
10 9 8 7 6 5 4 3 2

Library of Congress Cataloging-in-Publication Data

Smith, Charles W. G.
   The beginner's guide to edible herbs / by Charles W.G. Smith.
      p. cm.
   Includes index.
   ISBN 978-1-60342-528-5 (pbk. : alk. paper)
   1. Herbs. 2. Herb gardening. 3. Cookery (Herbs) I. Title.
SB351.H5S64 2010
635'.7—dc22
                           2010000845

The Beginner's Guide to

Edible Herbs

26 Herbs Everyone Should Grow & Enjoy

Charles W. G. Smith
introduction by Edward C. Smith

photography by Saxon Holt

Storey Publishing

CONTENTS

INTRODUCTION

by Edward C. Smith, author of The Vegetable Gardener's Bible

We call it "tomato sauce," but if all you found in it were tomatoes, you'd be mightily disappointed. Even if you added onions and some garlic, you'd still be a long way from what most of us expect to taste in a spoonful of tomato sauce. But add a pinch of thyme here and a teaspoon of oregano there, along with some finely minced fresh basil, and suddenly all sorts of taste buds start to tingle. Herbs make all the difference.

The term "herbs" encompasses many different kinds of plants, but they all have one thing in common: their various parts (usually the leaves and stems) are used for their scent or flavor, either in food or for medicinal purposes. Herbs are what moves many a sauce, soup, or salad dressing from ordinary to exceptional; an herb is often the special addition that makes an ethnic dish truly ethnic. It's hard to imagine cooking without them.

The good news is that you don't need to live near a specialty market to have access to fresh herbs, and you don't need to invest in those pricey (but tiny) jars of dried herbs. Most of what you need to put sparkle into your cooking you can grow right in your own backyard, along with the tomatoes, celery, squash, onions, carrots, and other vegetables you'll be cooking with. My wife, Sylvia, and I are always running out for a snip of this herb or a handful of that one while we're putting dinner together.

The Beginner's Guide to Edible Herbs is all about how to make herbs a part of your vegetable garden, many times in ways that benefit both the herbs and the vegetables. As a rule, herbs get along with vegetables in the garden as well as they do in the kitchen.

Finding a Home: Where to Plant the Herbs

Traditionally, herbs have been grown in a garden all their own. If you have the space and the inclination, it's just fine to grow them this way; many herbs are perennials and would therefore stay in

one spot year after year. Besides, if you're preparing soil and cultivating vegetable garden beds with power equipment, it's a real bother to maneuver around perennial plantings scattered among the vegetables. That's reason enough to isolate perennial herbs from the rest of the garden, or at least to plant them at the ends of beds. Herbs that are grown as annuals (cilantro, basil, parsley, savory) are easy enough to plant alongside vegetables in the garden, since you'll be harvesting them at the end of the season anyway.

What's Good for the Sauce Is Good for the Garden

In the kitchen, herbs will end up mixing with each other and with vegetables; there are good reasons for also letting them mix in the vegetable garden, where the intermingling may benefit both the herbs and the vegetables involved.

Gardeners through the ages have noticed that certain herbs — lemon balm, marjoram, and oregano, for example — appear to have a generally beneficial influence on other plants typically found in the vegetable garden. Basil, for example, is reputed to improve growth and enhance flavor of the tomatoes it grows near. Chives grown nearby may improve the flavor of carrots. And marjoram appears to have a beneficial effect on the flavor and growth of just about any garden plant it abuts.

Basil and parsley are both reputed to be good companions for asparagus. (But plant them at the ends of the asparagus

BEWARE THE GARDEN HUNS

Some herbs belie the measured growth habits that usually characterize the group; though gentle in appearance, they are conquerors in disguise, members in good standing of the gang I refer to as Garden Huns. Ignore one of these — any member of the large mint family, for example — for just a few weeks and it will colonize every bit of garden it can reach. And reach it will, more and more each year. Once they get a foothold, Garden Huns are very, very difficult to control. Forewarned is forearmed.

One option is to give these invasive sorts a "country" of their own, far from the vegetable or herb garden (preferably bordered by a sidewalk or some other kind of barrier). Another way to avoid being conquered by a Hun is to plant it in a pot, which is then placed in or near the garden, thereby gaining the benefits of companionable relationships (see What's Good for the Sauce Is Good for the Garden) while avoiding the consequences of invasion. And, yes, the potted mint will also be happy to grow indoors in the winter.

beds or in adjoining beds so they don't compete with the asparagus for nutrients.) Summer savory gets along fine with beans and corn, which also get along well with each other. Rosemary, dill, sage, and peppermint benefit any member of the large cabbage family (cabbage, Chinese cabbage, cauliflower, kale, broccoli, broccoli raab, kohlrabi, arugula, bok choy, radish, rutabaga, and turnip), but plant peppermint in a pot or in a nearby place all its own so that it doesn't take over the neighborhood. Carrots appear to like rosemary and sage, but not dill. Basil is as good a companion to tomatoes in the garden as it is in a tomato sandwich.

Over the eons that human beings have gardened, they've observed time and time again that some garden plants — many of them herbs — are rarely or never troubled by plant-eating insects. It may well have something to do with the strong taste and aroma that characterize most of the plants we call herbs. It turns out that these pest-free plants can confer some protection to plants normally prey to insect pests; other plants living within about 3 feet of pest-repellent plants may also be free of pests. Mints have the reputation of repelling all sorts of pests, including ants, cabbage worms, and even mice. Borage is supposed to repel tomato hornworms, as are rosemary, thyme, and sage.

On the flip side of the pest-repellent coin, there are herbs that actually *attract* pests, sometimes so well that the pests don't bother the plants that otherwise would have been their preferred hosts. Dill, for example, is reputed to be more attractive to tomato hornworms than tomatoes are! And that's not all the good news. Many herbs attract insects that are beneficial both to themselves and to

COMPANION PLANTING: MIRACLE OR MYTH?

Many of the supposedly beneficial relationships referred to as companion planting have not been proved scientifically, but neither has quite a bit of other garden lore. It is very difficult to "prove" a lot of what goes on in the garden because there are so many variables affecting outcomes. And many of the significant variables vary from garden to garden and even from year to year in the same garden. I tend to accept as likely to be true whatever plant/plant and plant/pest interactions have been observed and reported by many gardeners over the years. Yes, it may turn out that some of this is myth, but you're probably not hurting anything by following it, and you may even be making things better. Herbs are likely to end up near other garden plants anyway; they might as well end up where they could be doing some good.

other garden plants. Ladybugs and lace-wings, voracious eaters of aphids and other soft-bodied plant predators, are attracted by dill flowers. Borage is a magnet for butterflies, honey bees, and other pollinators. Where there is borage, there will always be plenty of pollinators to visit the other garden plants that need to be pollinated.

Tending and Attending

We'll get to the good news right away: herbs are generally pretty easy keepers. Put them in a place that suits them, and after that just do an occasional pruning (which doubles as a harvest) and make sure the plants get enough water.

The trick for success with herbs is to mimic as closely as you can the conditions that prevail in any particular herb's home region. For the many herbs of Mediterranean heritage, this means fairly minimal soil fertility and occasional shortages of water, conditions regularly encountered by plants living in that neck of the woods. Gardeners who also cook with herbs (and who have a better-developed sense of taste than I) claim that many herbs develop stronger flavor if they're not pampered too much. Occasional periods of drought may actually benefit herbs. A little stress builds character?

That said, in practice the herbs in our garden seem to do just fine in the same conditions that favor the vegetables growing there: good fertility, even watering, and a pH of 5.5 to 7.0. I can't see any reason not to plant a few herbs among the vegetables. (In fact, I like to grow some flowers there too, especially the edible ones, like nasturtiums and violas.)

HOW MANY PLANTS WILL YOU NEED?

Determining just how many of any one herb to grow depends a lot on your tastes and how big each plant grows. A single mint plant can spread so quickly that it can keep you in mint tea, mint jelly, mint potpourri, and mint vinegar all summer. However, a single plant of dill will only produce a few tablespoons of seeds. If you like to use dill frequently, you'll need a dozen or more plants to produce the supply you need. Here are some potential yields of some common herbs.

LIGHT YIELDS
Chamomile (flowers)
Chives (flowers)
Coriander (seeds)
Dill (seeds and foliage)

MEDIUM YIELDS
Basil (foliage)
Cilantro (foliage)
Rosemary (foliage)
Sage (foliage)
Summer savory (foliage)
Sweet marjoram (foliage)
Thyme (foliage)

ABUNDANT YIELDS
Catnip (foliage)
Chives (foliage)
English thyme (foliage)
Lemon balm (foliage)
Mint (foliage)
Oregano (foliage)

Text excerpted from *The Herb Gardener*, by Susan McClure (Storey Publishing, 1996)

It Is Seldom Indeed That Herbs Start from Seed

Many of the herbs we use in cooking are perennials; they may die back during the cold of winter, but the roots survive. As soon as spring heats things up a bit, new greenery pops forth and growth resumes. Tarragon, thyme, sage, oregano, chives, and the many sorts of mint are all perennials and usually survive winter's chill, especially if provided with a bit of protection — deep mulch or a cold frame or a grow tunnel of plastic. Bay Laurel (actually a small tree) and rosemary are perennials too but are much more sensitive to freezing temperatures; bring them indoors for the winter.

Perennial herbs, like other perennial garden plants, can be grown from seed but are usually propagated from cuttings. How come? Well, for starters, some herbs simply won't "come true" from seed (produce exactly the same plant from which the seed was gathered). Mints, which enjoy interbreeding, are a good example of this. So is tarragon; if grown from seed, it will produce a relatively tasteless plant (often called Russian tarragon). French tarragon — the tasty variant you want in your garden — is only propagated from cuttings, not from seed.

Some plants, like rosemary, *can* be started from seed but take a long time to reach a harvestable size. I'd recommend letting someone else tend to the birthing here; buy a well-started plant from a nursery or greenhouse. Sage is another good example; it will grow from seed, but it takes two years to grow a plant large enough to allow much of a harvest. The plants you buy at a nursery will already be a year old. When it comes to herbs, I tend to take the easy and scenic route; I buy most of them as started plants.

There are some herbs I do grow from seed, though, and would recommend to anyone interested in producing quantities of a certain herb. Prime example? Basil. It's easy to grow from seed, and we use enough of it at our house (in pesto, tomato sauce, and salads) that most of the seeds in a packet find an earthly home. Dill is another. Actually, after the first sowing of purchased seed, dill takes over the whole job and seeds itself. It's pretty much taken over part of a garden bed and appears in the spring according to its own schedule. All I need to do is thin and keep the patch weeded. Then, harvest; first the leaves for salads and dips, then green seed heads for pickles, and finally dry seeds. (Enough seeds always escape harvest to guarantee a bumper crop of dill the following spring.)

Harvest: A Way to Keep Things in Good Shape

Many herbs — basil and mint come to mind — benefit from periodic pruning. Clip off the tips of all the branches; this encourages the plant to become bushy rather than tall and lanky. It also postpones flowering, after which flavor may begin to decline.

If the leaves are what you're after (oregano, thyme, sage, marjoram, basil, mint), harvest them before the flowers emerge; the flavor and aroma are best then. If it's the seeds you want (dill, coriander), wait until the seeds have begun to turn brown, but before they start to fall from the plant.

Dry Now, Eat Later

Drying is more than just a good way to preserve the herb part of a garden's bounty; it also brings about some changes in the flavor and texture. Fresh-from-the-garden basil finely chopped and added to tomato sauce or salad dressing has a milder flavor but a stronger bouquet and a different "tooth" than dry basil. The same is true of parsley. Dried oregano and thyme, on the other hand, are stronger flavored than fresh.

The oils that make herbs what they are, providing both aroma and taste, are volatile — heat hastens their escape, and the higher the heat, the more rapid the escape. So the general rule for drying herbs is "warm but not hot." The oven at its lowest setting is okay for drying dill seeds but too warm for basil, thyme, or

marjoram leaves. The simplest method is to hang herb sprigs near (or from) the ceiling, perhaps over the refrigerator, where it's a little warmer than the rest of the room. Some herbs, such as bay laurel and borage, can also be dried in the refrigerator.

Freeze!
Stop Herbs at Their Best (and Keep Them That Way)

Drying, though it is the traditional and probably most often-used method for preserving herbs, is not the only way. Many herbs also freeze well, retaining most of their color and flavor, especially if they are already part of a sauce or a flavored butter when frozen. Frozen alone, in plastic bags, basil turns a very deep green, but it still makes an excellent pesto in the middle of winter. Herbs that do freeze well, which you'll learn more about later in this book, retain more of their "just picked" flavor and aroma than they do when dried.

In a pot, in a garden of their own, or right in among the vegetables whose tastes they'll enliven, herbs are easy to grow, easy to harvest, and easy to preserve for future use. And this is the book that tells you what you need to know: what to grow, where to grow it, and what to grow it near . . . or not so near.

26
Herbs
to Grow & Enjoy

Anise Hyssop

Agastache foeniculum

A relative of mint, anise hyssop is native to North and Central America. It thrived in the prairies and open spaces of the Great Plains, where native Americans used the leaves in teas to treat coughs. The Latin name, *Agastache*, comes from the Greek *agan,* meaning "very much," and *stachys,* meaning "ear of wheat," which is an accurate description of the spiky flower. The plants are stiffly erect, with dusky green leaves and spikes of small, bluish purple tubular flowers from July through September. With its long flowering period, tidy growth habit, and attractive flowers, anise hyssop makes an excellent addition to a perennial bed. The strongly aromatic leaves blend anise and peppermint scents. The blossoms attract bees, butterflies, and hummingbirds.

A Fragrant Purple Beauty

You can't miss the smell of anise hyssop on a stroll through the garden, and you wouldn't want to miss its beautiful bluish purple flowers.

GROW IT. Sow seeds either indoors in spring or on-site after danger of frost has passed, and transplant or thin plants to 12 inches apart. Water during periods of hot, dry weather; lower leaves can drop in late summer or during droughts. Propagate from seeds or by division in spring. Anise hyssop can be overwintered in colder areas of zone 4 and some sections of zone 3 by covering plants with a layer of mulch after the ground has frozen lightly.

HARVEST YOUR BOUNTY. For the strongest flavor grow plants in full sun in soil rich in organic matter, and harvest the leaves after flower buds appear but before they open. For subtler flavors grow in partial shade or harvest during bloom.

SOIL	Fertile, well drained
LIGHT	Full sun to light shade
PLANT TYPE	Perennial
HARDINESS	Zones 6-9

THE NOSE KNOWS BEST

Many of the herbs that find their way into our kitchens originated in the Mediterranean. Centuries of traditions have married tomatoes with basil, tarragon with carrots, dill with cucumbers. A few of our herbs, like anise hyssop, are outside that tradition. In this case, anise hyssop is a native of the Americas and has no firmly established role in Western cooking. So how do you decide what to do with an herb that has no established culinary tradition? Think with your nose!

Anise hyssop, for example, smells like a cross between root beer and licorice, which suggests that it would be good in beverages and desserts, which it is. Try it in pound cake for starters. But use anise hyssop sparingly; it is quite strongly flavored. Other herbs to try in pound cake include angelica, lavender, and rose geranium.

It's Good for What Ails You

The dried leaves of the plant make a sweet tea with healing properties. When you consume anise hyssop, it actually changes the chemical makeup of your saliva, making everything taste sweeter than normal.

USES. The dried or fresh leaves and flowers make an anise-flavored, slightly sweet tea that is said to help purify the body by inducing perspiration and is also useful in relieving congestion. Tender leaves gathered from growing tips are used in salads, while dried leaves make fine additions to sauces and potpourris.

PRESERVE FOR LATER. Dry leaves by hanging bunches by their stems until they're dry. Hang plants upside down in a well-ventilated, shaded, warm place. Leaves should dry in 2 to 5 days. Alternatively, spread a single layer of leaves on a paper towel and microwave on high for 1 to 3 minutes, checking every minute. Leaves are done when they feel dry but haven't lost any color. Store in airtight containers.

PART OF PLANT USED	Leaves
CULINARY COMPANIONS	Winter squash, fruit, ice cream, pound cake
USE TIP	It's surprisingly sweet, so add when sweetness is desirable.

SUN TEA

A wonderful way to begin to use herbs in tea is simply to place a handful of fresh sprigs in a gallon of water with five or six black-tea bags, and place this outside in the full sun for several hours to make "sun tea." Special glass jugs that have a spigot at the bottom of the jug and a screw-top lid are available for this purpose. Anise hyssop, lemon balm, lemon verbena, and all the mints work well in sun tea.

Making Herbal Teas

Some herbs make wonderful teas (anise hyssop, calendula, catnip, lavender, lemon balm, mint, to name a few), and you can create your own blends. You don't have to start with complex medicinal formulas. Get to know your herbs: how they taste, smell, and feel, and what blends well, and then experiment. Use stronger, primary flavors as the foundation, then add secondary herbs to create unique and interesting flavors, aromas, and textures.

Making mint tea bags

Cold Comfort

Herbs are well-known for their medicinal qualities. This tea is especially good when recovering from a really bad cold and is stronger because of the brewing process. Use fresh herbs if possible, or good-quality dried herbs. Be aware that the yarrow can cause heat flushing, good for breaking a fever.

- 1 part echinacea root
- 1 part peppermint leaves
- 1 part catnip leaves
- 1 part yarrow leaves
- 1 part lemon balm leaves

1. Put the echinacea in 1 quart of water and bring to a boil. Simmer, covered, for 20 minutes.

2. Add the rest of the herbs, stir well, cover, and steep 15 to 20 minutes.

3. Strain and add honey and lemon, if desired.

After-Dinner Tea

A simple, delicious, and very flavorful digestion-enhancing tea.

- 1 part spearmint leaves
- ⅛ part licorice root

Combine the herbs in a pot and cover with boiling water. Stir well, cover, and steep 15 to 20 minutes.

STEEP OR BOIL?

If you are using dried herb leaves, petals, or flowers, it is best to steep them. Start by bringing cold water just to the boiling point in a pan or teakettle, preferably an enameled one. You can put the tea directly into your teakettle and then strain before drinking, or you can use one of the many infusers sold to hold the loose tea. Pour boiling water over the tea and allow to steep for at least 5 minutes before tasting.

Because seed, bark, and peel oils are harder to release than those from leaves and flowers, it is best to boil, or decoct, them. Bring water to a boil on the stove. You can crush the seeds, bark, or whole spices before boiling, or pass them through a spice grinder. This will release the oils for maximum flavor. Add the crushed or whole seeds and other ingredients and simmer gently (use about 1 tablespoon of seeds for every 2 cups of water). Taste the tea after 5 minutes. Continue simmering and tasting until the tea is to your liking.

Basil

Ocimum basilicum

Basil species range from camphor basil, which is used as an insect repellent, to sacred basil, a plant grown in India for its protective influence. The most popular, however, is sweet basil, the leaves of which contain a variety of strongly aromatic oils in combinations that give the many different cultivars their distinctive scents: cinnamon basil (*O. basilicum* 'Cinnamon'), with spicy cinnamon-scented leaves; licorice basil (*O. basilicum* 'Anise'), with an earthy, anise aroma; and lemon basil (*O. basilicum* var. *citriodorum*), whose leaves bear rich scents of citrus. These and many others have become essential ingredients in the cuisine of countless cultures around the world.

A Fragrant Sun Lover

Each basil cultivar has a distinct scent, from cinnamon to lemon. Plant them in the sun, to ensure healthy plants and the full release of those aromatic oils.

GROW IT. Sow seeds indoors in early spring or on-site after night temperatures remain above 50°F. Once the plants are a few inches tall, thin them to 6 inches apart, and cover the soil around them with a light layer of screened mulch to retain moisture. Water the seedlings only as needed — keep the soil moist without overwatering. Basil prefers to dry out a little between waterings. Plant in a sunny spot so plants receive at least 6 hours of full sun every day. Pinch out growing tips to induce branching. Popular cultivars include 'Dark Opal', 'Purple Ruffles', and 'Genovese'.

HARVEST YOUR BOUNTY. Gather individual leaves anytime. To get the largest yield and best quality of leaves from your plants, pick leaves from the main stem or branches just below the suckers growing in the leaf nodes. For the best flavor, harvest basil just before the flowers develop. Prune by pinching off the flower buds with your fingers or snipping off the tops with scissors. To stimulate new growth, fertilize the plants with manure tea or fish emulsion after harvest, and in a few weeks you'll be able to pick again. Whole plants should be harvested as flowers begin to open.

SOIL	Fertile, evenly moist
LIGHT	Full sun
PLANT TYPE	Annual

PLAN TO HAVE ENOUGH

There are more than 60 basil cultivars available to gardeners around the world. Different cultivars are used for different purposes. Make sure you have enough for your needs: six plants for pesto and tomato seasoning, plus at least two each of the purple and scented varieties for making vinegars and oils and one plant each of the lettuce-leaf basils for summer salads and barbecue. Plan on a minimum of two of the bush basils for container growing throughout the year. Stagger your plantings for a continuous supply of fresh basil.

Beyond Tomatoes!

Basil and tomato is probably the most well-known herb-vegetable combination, but don't make short shrift of this herb. It works well with most any vegetable, and it even makes a nice tea.

USES. The entire plant is used, with the seeds, leaves, and flowers employed most often. The fresh or dried leaves are essential ingredients in tomato-based sauces and as a seasoning for vegetables, meats, and stuffings. A tea made from the leaves produces a warm, restorative feeling; itchy insect bites can be soothed by rubbing fresh leaves over the skin. Basil is said to aid digestion, relax cramps and muscle aches, and reduce fevers. In companion plantings, such as with tomatoes and peppers, it helps repel aphids.

PRESERVE FOR LATER. Fresh basil should not be placed in the refrigerator but rather in water on a windowsill. To dry basil, harvest clean, dry leaves (don't wash the leaves); tie in small bunches and hang upside down in a warm, dark place for 2 to 4 weeks. Alternatively, you could spread the leaves in a single layer on a cookie sheet and dry them in the oven on the lowest possible temperature for a few days. You could also freeze basil, although the leaves will turn black.

PART OF PLANT USED	Entire plant
CULINARY COMPANIONS	Garlic, onion, peppers, tomatoes
USE TIP	Add fresh basil at the end of cooking for best flavor.

Making Herbal Pesto

You can turn most herbs into pesto, an herb and oil paste flavored with nuts, garlic, and Parmesan. Herbs that work well include basil, chervil, chives, cilantro, dill, lovage, sweet marjoram, mint, sage, rosemary, or French tarragon. And once you've made that yummy green stuff, you can spread it on a pizza, douse it on salads or submarine sandwiches, dish it out over pasta, bake it into bread, or drizzle it over chicken roasted without the skin. Experiment! You'll be amazed by the pesto possibilities.

Basil Pesto

Here's a basic basil pesto recipe, but you could also experiment with adding sun-dried tomatoes or using opal or purple ruffles basil in place of the standard variety.

  2 cups fresh basil leaves
  ½ cup fresh parsley leaves
  ½ cup olive oil
  2 cloves garlic
    Salt and freshly ground black pepper
  ¼ cup roasted pine nuts (pignoli)
  ¼ cup freshly grated Parmesan or
    Asiago cheese

In a blender or food processor, puree the basil, parsley, oil, garlic, and salt and pepper to taste. Add the nuts and the cheese and process briefly until the pesto reaches the desired consistency.

MAKES 2 CUPS

Cilantro Pesto

Try this variation on the classic when you want to add a little heat to a dish.

2	teaspoons minced garlic
⅓	cup pine nuts or walnuts
⅓	cup olive oil
½	cup freshly grated Parmesan cheese
1	tablespoon freshly squeezed lime or lemon juice
1½	cups fresh cilantro leaves
1	serrano chile, seeded
	A little water (if needed)
	Salt

1. Put all the ingredients except the water and salt in a blender or food processor.

2. Run the machine until everything is smooth, adding a bit of water if needed. Add salt to taste.

MAKES ABOUT 1½ CUPS

Pesto Tomato Pasta

Here basil pesto combines with summer's best tomatoes and rotelle for a tasty treat.

¾	cup extra-virgin olive oil
½	cup balsamic vinegar
2	cups fresh basil leaves
½	cup fresh parsley leaves
4	large cloves garlic
	Salt and freshly ground black pepper
8	large tomatoes, peeled and cut into quarters
1	pound rotelle or other pasta
½	cup Parmesan cheese

1. Put a large pot of water on the stove to boil.

2. Place the oil and vinegar in a food processor and add the basil, parsley, garlic, and salt and pepper to taste. Puree.

3. Add the tomatoes and process until they are coarsely chopped.

4. Cook the pasta in boiling water according to the directions on the package. Drain.

5. While the pasta is hot, add the tomato mixture and toss gently. Serve immediately with the Parmesan while the pasta is still warm.

SERVES 6 TO 8

Bay Laurel

Laurus nobilis

Bay laurel is a woody shrub native to southern Europe, the Azores, and the Canary Islands. Under optimum conditions it grows into a tree up to 50 feet high. The glossy, evergreen leaves are leathery and pleasantly aromatic. In spring, inconspicuous yellow flowers blossom in the axils of the leaves, followed later by dark purple berries. Its Latin name translates to "noble victory"; historically, garlands of bay were draped over the heads of notable Romans. Bay laurel continues to be used as a symbol of accomplishment. In slow-cooked sauces, stews, and braises, bay leaves impart a sweet, pungent flavor, with hints of nutmeg, vanilla, and pine. The dried leaves can impart a bitterness, so add with caution. The leaves should be removed before serving.

A Tender Tree

In warm regions, this evergreen shrub can be grown outdoors and may grow as tall as 50 feet. In cold climates it will need winter protection.

GROW IT. In warm regions bay laurel is sometimes grown from seeds, though germination can take up to a year. A better method of propagation is to either transplant suckers from mature plants or air-layer the stems. In northern regions, bay laurel is commonly grown in pots filled with a fertile growing medium, such as California mix. Transplant to larger pots as the plant grows, and overwinter in a warm, sunny spot away from cold drafts. Varieties include 'Angustifolia', with willow-shaped leaves, and 'Aurea', with golden foliage.

HARVEST YOUR BOUNTY. Pick leaves anytime.

SOIL	Fertile, well drained
LIGHT	Full sun to partial shade
PLANT TYPE	Evergreen shrub
HARDINESS	Zones 8–10

Dry and Flavorful

Most herbs lose some of their flavor when dried, but the opposite is true for bay: its flavor intensifies through the drying process.

USES. The large leaves of bay laurel not only flavor soups, stews, and sauces but also aid in digestion. Fresh leaves may be used in recipes, though dried ones have an even stronger flavor and remain flavorful for about a year. A tonic made from the leaves is used to treat dandruff. Commercially, figs are packed in bay leaves to repel insects.

PRESERVE FOR LATER. To dry in the microwave, place the leaves on paper towels for 1 to 3 minutes, checking every minute. To dry in the refrigerator, gently wash the leaves in cool water and allow their surface moisture to evaporate. Place leaves in a fine-mesh bag and hang from a hook, or place in an uncovered bowl and stir daily. Leaves will be dry in 2 to 7 days.

PART OF PLANT USED	Leaves
CULINARY COMPANIONS	Pot roasts, beef stews, tomato sauce
USE TIP	Store dried leaves in the refrigerator.

AN IDEAL CONTAINER PLANT

Slow-growing bay laurel is an ideal plant for a large container — at least for its first five years — because it grows so slowly, about 1 foot per year. If you live where winters are mild (temperatures are above 25°F year-round), it can stay outside on a deck or patio. Otherwise, you will have to bring the plant in for the winter.

Bay laurel thrives on neglect. In fact, overwatering, especially in the winter, is the worst thing you can do. Prune off the tip of the plant to encourage a shrubby, branching habit. Then just pluck leaves from the tree as you need them.

Making a Bouquet Garni

Used to flavor soups, stews, and broths, a bouquet garni is a group of herbs either tied together with kitchen twine or placed in a cheesecloth bag. The classic combination is bay leaf, thyme, and parsley (the proportions vary according to the soup, stew, or broth you are making). The herbs are removed before serving.

Beta Soup

For this soup, make a bouquet garni with 1 bay leaf, 2 sprigs fresh thyme, 2 sprigs fresh oregano, and 4 sprigs fresh parsley. The herbs harmonize the flavors of the vegetables and create a complex, wonderful broth.

1   tablespoon canola or olive oil
2   cups diced yellow onions
¼   cup thinly sliced lovage stems
2   cloves garlic, minced
1½ cups thinly sliced carrots
1   cup peeled and diced sweet potatoes
1   cup peeled and diced winter squash
1   cup peeled, seeded, and chopped
    tomatoes
4   cups vegetable stock or canned
    vegetable broth
½   cup dry white wine
1   bouquet garni
½   pound green beans, cut into 1-inch
    lengths, or one 10-ounce package
    frozen green beans, thawed
½   pound fresh kale, spinach, or Swiss
    chard, washed and chopped
1   cup spinach rotelle or elbow pasta

1. In a large saucepan, heat the oil over medium heat. Add the onions and cook, stirring occasionally, for 3 to 5 minutes, or until soft. Add the lovage and garlic and cook for 30 seconds.

2. Add the carrots, sweet potatoes, squash, tomatoes, stock, wine, and bouquet garni. Bring to a simmer, stirring occasionally. Reduce the heat to low, cover, and cook for 30 minutes, or until the vegetables are tender.

3. Add the beans, greens, and pasta. Raise the heat to medium and cook for 15 minutes, or until the pasta is done. Remove the bouquet garni and serve immediately.

SERVES 6

Bee Balm

Monarda didyma

When colonists protested the use of the English tea tax by insti-
gating the infamous Boston Tea Party and forswearing the use
of English tea, they satisfied their craving for tea by brewing bee
balm leaves, a trick taught to the settlers by the Oswego Indians,
hence one of the alternative names of the plant: Oswego tea. Bee
balm is as much at home in the perennial border as it is in the herb
garden. Native to much of eastern North America, it forms thick
colonies in wetlands and along streambanks. Plants have tall, pliant, four-sided stems draped with aromatic, dusky green leaves
and crowned with a distinctive cluster of scarlet flowers in summer. Bee balm attracts butterflies and hummingbirds. There are
more than 50 commercial cultivars and hybrids.

Something to Buzz About

The tubular scarlet flowers of bee balm attract not only bees, but also butterflies, hummingbirds, and other nectar-seeking creatures.

GROW IT. Grow from seeds sown indoors or from purchased transplants. Plants spread very quickly once they're established and should be divided every 3 years. Bee balm is an excellent plant for a wet meadow. Plant in an area with good air circulation to inhibit powdery mildew, which often appears on the leaves in late summer. There are many excellent cultivars of bee balm: The rich red flowers of 'Cambridge Scarlet' have made it a longtime favorite.

'Raspberry Wine' has scarlet flowers with lilac undertones and resists powdery mildew. 'Marshall's Delight' blooms from July into September and was bred for those who can't get enough of bee balm's unique scarlet flowers.

HARVEST YOUR BOUNTY. Pick small leaves just before the flower buds open. Pluck the petals off the flower's center and sprinkle on salads.

SOIL	Rich, evenly moist
LIGHT	Full sun to light shade
PLANT TYPE	Perennial
HARDINESS	Zones 4–8

COMMON NAMES CAN BE CONFUSING

Like many popular garden plants, *Monarda didyma* has many common names, including bergamot, scarlet bee balm, scarlet monarda, crimson bee balm, and Oswego tea. Bergamot is the flavoring associated with Earl Grey tea, but the herb that actually flavors the tea is *Citrus bergamia*. What the two plants share is a certain aroma, which is defined as "bergamot" — a lemony, minty odor.

Meanwhile, another plant, *Monarda fistulosa*, is known as "wild bergamot" or horsemint. *Monarda punctara* is also known as horsemint. All of the monardas are quite similar. They are lovely in the garden and quite attractive to bees and hummingbirds.

Teas and More

Although also called bergamot, bee balm is not to be confused with the flavoring for Earl Grey tea. Nonetheless, the dried leaves are used in herbal teas.

USES. The petals taste surprisingly like oregano and can be sprinkled on salads or pizza as it comes out of the oven. Or you can add the petals to herb butters (see page 120) or herbed goat cheese (page 44). Infusions made from bee balm are used to treat colds, sore throats, headaches, upset stomachs, nausea, menstrual pain, and insomnia. Inhaling the steam produced by combining the leaves with boiling water can help relieve sore throats.

PRESERVE FOR LATER. Dry in the refrigerator to preserve flavor by spreading an even layer of leaves and flowers on a baking sheet covered with paper towels, hanging in a fine-mesh bag, or placing in an uncovered bowl and stirring daily. Leaves and flowers will dry in 2 to 7 days. Harvest and dry plants in small bunches (hung upside down in a well-ventilated, shaded, warm place) for use in dried arrangements.

PART OF PLANT USED	Leaves and flowers
CULINARY COMPANIONS	Tomatoes, red meats, rosemary, thyme
USE TIP	Pick small leaves before flowers open and pick petals in full bloom.

Borage

Borago officinalis

Borage is native to Europe and has been used and cultivated since ancient times. Its name stems from a Latin word that means "hairy garment" — a reference to the plant's coarsely hairy leaves. Borage is reputed to lift the spirits, induce euphoria, and even create a feeling of courage in those who eat it. Recent research has determined that borage does indeed stimulate the production of adrenaline — which just might account for the sense of well-being and courage some people feel after nibbling on the plant. The plant has a mild cucumber-like flavor that is somewhat more noticeable in the young, tender leaves than in the flowers. Delicate, blue-starred borage blossoms make a stunning garnish, especially because it is one of the very few blue-colored edibles.

True-Blue Beauty

Borage is one of the only truly blue flowers you can grow, and because it self-sows, you will have many of these blue beauties in your garden.

GROW IT. Sow indoors in early spring or outdoors after danger of frost has passed. Borage develops a taproot rather quickly, and transplanting should be done carefully so that the root is not damaged. Pinch plants back when they are 6 inches tall to encourage bushiness. In midsummer, prune them back by one-half; they will produce a new crop of tender leaves that can be harvested in late summer. Support plants that grow to over 2 feet in height.

Borage often self-seeds; volunteers that appear the following spring should be transplanted before the taproot gets too big. The variety 'Alba' has snow white flowers, while 'Variegata' has gray-green leaves laced with white.

HARVEST YOUR BOUNTY. Gather leaves and flowers anytime. The beautiful starlike lavender-blue flowers appear from midsummer until frost.

SOIL	Rich, evenly moist, well drained
LIGHT	Full sun to partial shade
PLANT TYPE	Annual

DON'T FILL UP ON FLOWERS

The herb garden yields lots of edible flowers that make outstanding garnishes. Indeed, with the exception of French tarragon, all edible herbs produce blossoms that can be eaten. But do use these edible blossoms sparingly; the flavor can be quite overwhelming. Think petals rather than whole blossoms, with the possible exception of tiny blossoms such as borage.

Edible blossoms also include daylilies (dried daylily buds are called golden needles and are found in Chinese stir-fries), meadowsweet, violas, nasturtiums, pinks, roses, tulips (taste like raw peas), and violets.

A Cucumber-like Treat

Use borage sparingly in salads and teas. Both the blooms and leaves can be added to Bloody Marys. The delicate blue blossoms can be used to garnish soups, desserts, or drinks.

USES. The tender leaves have a delicate, cucumber-like flavor. Add them to salads, lightly steam like spinach, or sauté in butter. The flowers are a tasty and colorful addition to salads; traditionally, they have been added to wine as well. A tea made from the leaves and flowers is said to relieve coughs and ease the discomfort of colds. Use borage as an accent — but in moderation, as some authorities suggest that large amounts of it may cause liver damage.

PRESERVE FOR LATER. Dry leaves and flowers in the microwave (a single layer on paper towels, microwaved on high for 1 to 3 minutes) or in the refrigerator on a baking sheet covered in paper towels, hanging in a mesh bag, or stirred daily in an uncovered bowl. Drying can take 2 to 7 days in the fridge.

PART OF PLANT USED	Leaves and flowers
CULINARY COMPANIONS	Strawberries, tomatoes
USE TIP	When steamed, the furry coating on the leaves disappears.

Making Juices with Herbs

Appetizing and healthful, fruit and vegetable juices are refreshing on their own, but with the addition of herbs, they provide even more pleasure and health-giving properties.

SUGGESTED COMBINATIONS

- Apple juice with sage or thyme
- Berry juice with mint
- Carrot juice with marjoram or tarragon
- Celery juice with lovage, parsley, or chives
- Cherry juice with lavender
- Cranberry juice with rosemary
- Grape juice with thyme
- Grapefruit juice with anise hyssop
- Papaya juice with marjoram
- Peach or nectarine juice with coriander
- Tomato juice with basil or borage

Use 1 teaspoon of fresh herbs for 1 cup of juice. To blend: With an electric juice extractor, add herbs as the juice is being made or just afterward. For store-bought juices, add fresh herbs 30 minutes before serving.

At left, ice cubes laced with borage flowers

Cranberry Punch with Lavender and Rosemary

Use this recipe as a basis for experimenting with other fruit juices and herbs. Health-food stores abound with juices not often seen in groceries, but don't overlook basics such as pineapple juice or the different cranberry mixtures.

- ¼ cup fresh rosemary leaves
- 1 tablespoon dried lavender flowers
- 2 sticks cinnamon
- 6 whole cloves
- 1 quart cranberry juice

1. Combine the rosemary, lavender, cinnamon, and cloves in a small saucepan with 2½ cups water. Bring to a boil over high heat, then reduce heat to low and simmer for 5 minutes.

2. Remove from the heat and let steep for 5 minutes. Strain and combine with the juice in a pitcher. Refrigerate and serve cold, or heat and serve warm.

MAKES 1½ QUARTS

Orange, Melon, and Borage Cooler

This is a nice way to cool off, and the pretty borage flowers make it a lovely treat to serve guests.

- 2 cups small, tender fresh borage leaves
- 3 cups melon chunks, seeds removed
- 1 cup orange juice
- 2 tablespoons sugar
- 6 ice cubes
- ½ cup plain nonfat yogurt

1. Freeze ½ cup of the borage leaves in ice cube trays the night before.

2. Combine the rest of the borage leaves with the remaining ingredients in a blender and puree. Pour into glasses, add a couple of borage ice cubes to each glass for garnish, and serve immediately.

MAKES 1 QUART

Making Ketchups

With the addition of different herbs (and even different fruits!), ketchup can be so much more than a one-dimensional red sauce. The first-known recipe for tomato ketchup was published in 1812. Before that, ketchup, or catsup, was a spicy, soy-based condiment. The name itself is derived from the Malay-Chinese word kechap, *a salty, fish-based condiment similar to one used by the Romans. Today, ketchups are cooked sauces used as condiments, made with fruits or vegetables, vinegar, sugar, and spices.*

Quick Tomato Ketchup

The classic you can make at home. Plain cider vinegar can be substituted for homemade lovage cider vinegar.

3½ cups (28 ounces) canned tomato
     sauce
⅓ cup honey
⅓ cup lovage cider vinegar
2 tablespoons minced onion
1 clove garlic, minced
1 teaspoon salt
½ teaspoon freshly ground black
     pepper
½ teaspoon dry mustard
⅛ teaspoon ground cayenne pepper
⅛ teaspoon ground allspice
⅛ teaspoon ground cloves
⅛ teaspoon ground coriander seeds

In a large nonreactive saucepan, combine all the ingredients and place over low heat. Stirring frequently, simmer until the mixture reaches the consistency of commercial ketchup, or about 30 minutes. Pour into hot, sterilized ketchup bottles and refrigerate when cool.

MAKES TWO 13- OR 14-OUNCE BOTTLES

Mushroom Ketchup

Use this as a condiment for roasts, steaks, hamburgers, and chops as well as a seasoning for sauces, gravies, and salad dressings.

3 pounds mushrooms, thinly sliced

2 tablespoons non-iodized salt

1 cup chopped onion

1 small hot red chile, seeded and chopped

2 cloves garlic, minced

1 tablespoon fresh thyme, chopped

1 tablespoon fresh parsley, chopped

1 tablespoon fresh marjoram, chopped

½ teaspoon ground allspice

½ teaspoon ground ginger

¼ teaspoon ground cloves

1 bay leaf

1 cup mixed-herb or mixed-spice sherry vinegar

2 tablespoons honey

1. Put the mushrooms and salt in a nonreactive bowl, mixing thoroughly. Cover and let mixture stand at room temperature for 24 hours, stirring occasionally.

2. Puree the mushrooms in a food processor or food mill, then pour into a large nonreactive kettle.

3. Combine the remaining ingredients, except the bay leaf, in a blender and process until smooth. Stir into the pureed mushrooms, mixing well. Add the bay leaf.

4. Place over medium-high heat and bring to a boil. Reduce the heat to low and simmer, uncovered, and stir frequently for 1 to 2 hours, or until the ketchup is very thick. Remove the bay leaf.

MAKES 4 TO 5 HALF-PINT JARS

Calendula

Calendula officinalis

A welcome addition to any flower garden, calendula has lance-shaped medium green leaves and bright yellow or orange daisy-like blossoms that bloom from summer until a killing frost. Although an annual, the flower self-seeds readily. Its name comes from a Latin word meaning "first day of the month" and refers to the plant's long bloom time. Calendula is also known as pot marigold because English cooks used to throw one blossom into a pot to thicken and color soups and stews. But don't confuse this plant with marigolds (*Tagetes* spp.), which the English call "African marigolds," or marsh marigolds (*Caltha palustris*), because they are completely different plants.

A Lasting Bloom

As a bonus, calendula makes an excellent cut flower. Cut the flowers when the blooms are almost fully open and recut stems underwater to make flowers last nearly a week in a vase.

GROW IT. In zones 8 through 10, sow seeds outdoors in fall; in other zones, seeds can be started indoors 2 months before last frost or outdoors after the danger of frost has passed. Set plants 1 to 2 feet apart, depending on the height of the mature plant, and mulch around them to retain soil moisture and keep roots cool. Cut back spent flowers as they appear. Calendulas are sensitive to heat and crowding; in hot regions, plants may die in midsummer.

They benefit from light afternoon shade in the South, as well as sites with good air circulation. Many varieties are available, ranging from compact, dwarf forms to tall types. Calendulas are sometimes bothered by aphids, slugs, leafhoppers, or whiteflies.

HARVEST YOUR BOUNTY. Pick flowers when they are dry and about three-quarters of the way open.

SOIL	Fertile, well drained
LIGHT	Full sun to very light shade
PLANT TYPE	Annual

DEADHEADING

To keep your herb foliage fresh and also to encourage a second period of bloom for some herbs, such as calendula, remove the faded flowers on any herb except those you harvest for seed. This is called "deadheading." For ornamentals such as calendula, cut the old flowers off just above young flower buds developing lower on the stem.

A Less-Expensive Saffron

Calendula petals lend a nice yellow color to dishes. You may even find them in desserts.

USES. Calendula has a long history of use as a medicinal herb added to skin creams and shampoos. The petals are used as a substitute for saffron, imparting a rich, golden yellow color to rice dishes, soups, breads, cheese spreads, and butter.

PRESERVE FOR LATER. Dry the petals in a cool, shady place, with good air circulation, on absorbent paper. Dried petals and flowers can be stored in jars.

PART OF PLANT USED	Flowers
CULINARY COMPANIONS	Cheese, eggs
USE TIP	Use petals as a garnish or saffron substitute. They have a mild, peppery flavor.

Making Herbal Desserts

Herbs for dessert? You'll find that herbs can succeed in the unlikeliest of dishes — including cookies and cakes. They will often impart a distinct aroma that is at once unexpected and comforting, and the color of their flowers can make an everyday dessert extra-special. But a word of caution: If you have planned a heavily herbed soup, or you're serving a chicken dish doused in oregano, you might want to steer clear of thyme sorbet or anise cookies. Too much enthusiasm may frazzle the palate.

Crisp Caraway Cookies

Caraway seeds bring a distinctive taste to many breads, cakes, and cookies. The leaves of the plant are mild tasting, usually used in soups, but less common than the crunchy seeds.

1⅔ cups unbleached flour
1 teaspoon baking powder
¼ teaspoon baking soda
¼ teaspoon salt
2 teaspoons caraway seeds
½ cup (1 stick) butter or margarine, softened
⅔ cup sugar
2 eggs
½ teaspoon vanilla extract

1. Preheat the oven to 375°F.

2. Mix together the flour, baking powder, baking soda, salt, and caraway seeds in a small bowl. Set aside.

3. Cream the butter and sugar in a large bowl until fluffy. Add the eggs and vanilla, and beat well.

4. Stir in the flour mixture. Wrap the dough in plastic wrap and chill several hours, overnight, or until firm enough to roll (the dough will still be rather soft).

5. Cut the dough into quarters. Remove one quarter at a time from the refrigerator. Roll the dough very thin on a floured surface. (Use a pastry cloth and covered rolling pin to prevent the dough from sticking.) Cut with a floured 3-inch round cutter. Put on ungreased cookie sheets.

6. Bake on the top rack of the oven 8 to 10 minutes, watching closely. Remove to a wire rack to cool. Store cooled cookies in an airtight container or freezer.

MAKES 4 DOZEN COOKIES

Lemon Cheesecake with Calendula Blossoms

The blossoms of some herbs are just so beautiful, you can't help but want to bring that color and vibrancy into the kitchen. Calendulas are often used as a way to add color to cheese or cakes. Finely ground calendula petals can be added to this cheesecake for color and a few petals or blossoms used as a garnish on each serving.

6	eggs, separated
½	cup (1 stick) plus 2 tablespoons butter, softened
½	cup plus 2 tablespoons sugar
12	ounces cream cheese, softened
4	teaspoons chopped fresh lemon balm leaves or 2 teaspoons dried
4	teaspoons finely grated lemon zest
2	teaspoons finely ground calendula petals

1. Preheat the oven to 325°F. Grease a 10-inch angel food tube pan.

2. In a small mixer bowl, beat the egg whites until they stand in soft peaks.

3. In another large bowl, cream the butter, sugar, egg yolks, and cream cheese. Add the lemon balm, lemon zest, and petals to the butter mixture. Fold in the beaten egg whites.

4. Scrape into the prepared pan and bake 55 minutes. Cool 10 minutes before inverting on a plate.

SERVES 10

Lemon Thyme Cookies

You can use another variety of thyme.

1	cup (2 sticks) butter or margarine, softened
1½	cups sugar
2	eggs
2½	cups unbleached flour
1	teaspoon cream of tartar
½	teaspoon salt
5	tablespoons finely chopped fresh lemon thyme or 3 tablespoons dried

1. In a large bowl, cream the butter with the sugar, add the eggs, and mix well.

2. In a small bowl, sift together the flour, cream of tartar, and salt. Stir the flour mixture into the butter, sugar, and eggs until well blended, then add the lemon thyme.

3. Chill overnight or until firm enough to roll.

4. Preheat the oven to 350°F. Roll the chilled dough into 1-inch balls and bake on a greased cookie sheet for 10 minutes.

MAKES 4 DOZEN COOKIES

Caraway

Carum carvi

Caraway is one of the most ancient of cultivated plants and has been grown for well over 5,000 years. The plants have upright, hollow stems and deeply cut leaves that resemble those of carrots. During the first season, the plant produces a rich display of foliage. The following spring a flush of new foliage appears, followed by a 2- to 4-foot stem topped by an umbel of small white or pink flowers. A few weeks after the flowers fade, the small, tasty seeds ripen and can be collected. Caraway seeds have been used since ancient times and were brought to Spain by the Moors. Today, the seeds are closely associated with breads. They are also used to flavor cabbage, cheese, and sausage dishes.

Attract the Good Bugs

Caraway's ferny foliage attracts beneficial insects like lacewings, hoverflies, and parasitic mini-wasps. These "good bugs" will eat the bugs that do damage to your garden.

GROW IT. Sow seeds directly in the garden about 2 weeks before the last frost. Gently press the seeds into the soil surface and cover lightly with vermiculite. Thin seedlings to stand 6 to 12 inches apart. Caraway does not like to be transplanted or disturbed. Fertilize lightly when seedlings are 3 inches tall and again the following season when the flower shoot appears. Once established, the plants are drought tolerant and usually do not need much watering.

HARVEST YOUR BOUNTY. Cut flower heads as seeds begin to turn from a yellowish color to brown.

SOIL	Well drained, fertile
LIGHT	Full sun
PLANT TYPE	Biennial
HARDINESS	Zones 3–8

SOWING SEEDS OUTDOORS

The easiest way to deal with seeds is to sow them directly in the soil. Plant twice as many seeds as you need. If the temperature, moisture, and soil are right, many will come up; if they all sprout, you can pull every other one out or move them elsewhere.

1. Prepare the soil carefully before direct-sowing. You need a fine, light soil that lets seedlings emerge easily.
2. Plant seeds when soil temperatures are right for them. Cool-season herbs (such as parsley and cilantro) favor cool soil, and warm-season herbs (such as basil) prefer warm soil.

Not for Bread Alone

Caraway seeds are probably most well-known for their appearance in rye breads, but the leaves and seeds are great in a variety of dishes.

USES. Use the seeds to flavor breads, cheese, meat, and vegetable dishes or cookies. Chewing a few seeds is said to relieve indigestion. The fresh leaves can be gathered anytime; chopped and sprinkled over salads, they add a distinctive zing. Also, the taproot, which looks like a white carrot, is edible and very nutritious.

PRESERVE FOR LATER. Hang stems upside down in a paper bag to catch seeds as they fall. Place seeds in a sieve, and pour boiling water over them. Dry the seeds in a sunny place for a few days, and store in a sealed jar.

PART OF PLANT USED	Seeds, leaves, and taproot
CULINARY COMPANIONS	Cabbage, rye bread, cheese, sausage
USE TIP	Lightly toast the seeds to enhance the flavor.

3. Check directions on the seed packet for depth and spacing.
4. Plant herbs in straight or double rows for edgings or for cutting in a vegetable garden. Or thinly sprinkle quick-growing annuals such as dill and basil across wide beds. Thin the young plants to use in salads or for seasonings, leaving the remaining herbs enough room to mature.
5. Label the seeded area well so you know which plants are your herbs.
6. Keep the seeded area moist. If the weather is dry, sprinkle gently with a fine mist so you don't wash smaller seeds away.

Making Herbal Cheeses

Herbal cheeses are a wonderful party food, but you can also use them to make everyday foods like cheese sandwiches special. To make, wash fresh herbs and pat them dry. Chop them finely, add a bit of lemon juice, and mix into soft, room-temperature cheese. If the cheese is too firm, blend it with some yogurt or cream cheese. You can mix the herbs and cheese by hand (if you grate the hard cheese first) or puree them together in the food processor. You can also form the cheese into small balls and roll them in herbs, combined with nuts and oil if you wish. Refrigerate herbal cheeses for a few hours, at least, so the flavors can mix.

Herb-Marinated Goat Cheese

Adaptable to many cooking uses, fresh goat cheese may be best appreciated as an appetizer or snack when simply marinated with herbs — especially basil, thyme, rosemary, marjoram, chives, or fennel. Use both fresh leaves and flowers for the marinade and as a garnish.

- 8 ounces fresh goat cheese
- 2 tablespoons whole or coarsely chopped fresh herb leaves or edible flowers
- 10 black, green, or white peppercorns
  Extra-virgin olive oil

1. Cut cheese into ½-inch-thick slices. In a glass jar, layer slices with herbs and peppercorns. Cover with olive oil and attach the lid.

2. Let sit for at least a day to allow the flavors to blend. This will stay fresh for about a week at room temperature. If desired, store in the refrigerator, bringing to room temperature before serving.

MAKES 8 OUNCES

Herb Cheese Spread

Try this cheesy mix on a crusty heel of whole wheat or oatmeal bread, five minutes out of the oven. Experiment and use different herbs, such as thyme or rosemary, in place of the caraway and chives. And if your guests are really young, you can always omit the alcohol.

- ½ cup (1 stick) butter, softened
- 3 cups grated cheddar cheese
- 2 tablespoons finely snipped fresh chives
- 1 tablespoon caraway seeds
- 2 tablespoons cognac

1. Beat the butter and cheese together in a large bowl.

2. Blend in the chives, caraway seeds, and cognac.

MAKES ABOUT 2 CUPS

Cheese with fresh thyme leaves

Catnip

Nepeta cataria

Catnip has been famous since ancient times for its intoxicating effects on cats. Cats will ignore a patch of catnip growing in the garden, only reacting when the leaves are bruised or dried. In addition to appealing to cats, catnip is considered good for preventing colds. A member of the mint family, catnip tastes mildly minty. A rather rangy herb with an open growth habit, it has semi-erect stems ornamented with rough-textured, pungently aromatic foliage and spikes of small white flowers bedecked with tiny purple spots. Catmint (*Nepeta* × *faasennii*), a more ornamental relative of catnip, is attractive enough for the perennial border but lacks catnip's potent medicinal qualities.

A Substitute for Lavender

The purple variety of catnip is a great alternative to lavender in the garden. It isn't as fussy, and it reblooms if you cut it back.

GROW IT. Sow seeds indoors in spring and transplant to the garden, or direct-sow after danger of frost has passed. Space or thin the plants to 18 inches apart and cover the soil with a light layer of compost or well-rotted manure. Fertilize lightly every few weeks with an organic fertilizer. As soon as the first flowers fade, cut the plants back by half to encourage them to bloom again.

Catnip is a very vigorous grower and once established can become invasive; bury plant guards around plantings to inhibit its spread.

HARVEST YOUR BOUNTY. Gather the fresh, tender leaves anytime before the plant flowers. In late summer, gather the topmost leaves.

SOIL	Sandy, well drained
LIGHT	Full sun to partial shade
PLANT TYPE	Perennial
HARDINESS	Zones 4–9

HOW BIG SHOULD MY POT BE?

Here are suggestions for appropriate pot size for different kinds of herbs and stages of growth.

4-INCH POT: Small thyme division, basil seedling, sweet marjoram seedling, or any young nursery plants intended for transplanting

6-INCH POT: Bush basil, chives, parsley, sweet marjoram, oregano, thyme, summer savory. Note that most herbs won't stay in a 6-inch pot more than 6 to 8 months. Be prepared to transplant perennial herbs into larger containers as necessary.

8-INCH POT: Sweet basil, dill, sage

12-INCH POT: Bronze fennel, lavender, mints, young lemon verbena

LARGER POTS: Mature rosemary, bay tree, lemon verbena

It's Good for People, Too

Cats may go wild for the stuff, but people who know the medicinal benefits of catnip can't resist the stuff either. It makes a great tea and a fine addition to sauces and stews.

USES. Fresh leaves add a nip to salads or make a softly flavored, relaxing tea. The leaves can also be finely minced to add an undertone of mint to sauces or hearty stews. A tea from the dried leaves is said to relieve the discomforts of indigestion, fevers, colds, and the flu, as well as to induce relaxing sleep. 'Citriodora' is a cultivar with aromatic, lemon-scented leaves that makes an even more flavorful tea than the species.

And, of course, cloth pouches liberally filled with catnip are a turn-on to cats.

PRESERVE FOR LATER. Dry leaves on a screen in a cool, dry place. Depending on the temperature of the air and the air's circulation, the leaves should be dry in 2 to 5 days. If the leaves turn black or mold begins to grow on them, discard the batch. Store dried leaves in airtight containers.

PART OF PLANT USED	Leaves
CULINARY COMPANIONS	None
USE TIP	Add young leaves to salads and teas.

DEHYDRATORS

Dehydrators take the guesswork out of drying herbs, particularly tender leaves such as basil and mint. Preheat the dehydrator with the thermostat set between 95°F and 115°F. Rinse the herbs under cool, running water, shake to remove excess moisture, and arrange in a single layer on the dehydrator trays. Drying times may vary from 1 to 4 hours. Check periodically. Herbs are dry when the leaves crumble. Check your instruction booklet for details.

Making Herbal Jellies and Jams

Piquant jellies and jams can be made with any number of fresh herbs: basil, lemon verbena, marjoram, mint, parsley, rosemary, sage, tarragon, or thyme. Use them singly or combine them. Lemon verbena and mint, for instance, live together nicely, as do basil and parsley. Sage and cilantro, on the other hand, would clash.

Herb jellies make wonderful fillings for tea sandwiches, combining well with sweet butter or fresh goat cheese or cream cheese. They also complement roasted or grilled meats. Of course, herb jellies are delightful with biscuits, breads, and muffins, even peanut butter sandwiches!

Basic Herb Jelly

This basic recipe can be used for any herb or pleasant herbal combination.

2½   cups boiling water
1   cup fresh herbs, leaves and stems,
     plus 10 leaves for garnish
4½   cups sugar
¼   cup lemon juice or vinegar
½   bottle liquid pectin

1. In a medium, nonreactive saucepan, pour the boiling water over the herbs, cover, and let stand for 20 minutes.

2. Add the sugar and lemon juice to the infusion. Heat until the sugar dissolves. Bring the mixture to a boil and add the pectin. Boil for 1 minute, stirring constantly.

3. Remove from the heat and skim off the foam. Place a few fresh herb leaves into each jelly jar. Pour the jelly into hot, sterilized jars with two-piece canning lids, leaving ½ inch of headspace. Process 5 minutes in a boiling-water-bath canner. Adjust for altitude, if necessary.

MAKES 4 HALF-PINT JARS

Hot Pepper Jam

A southern favorite served with cream cheese and crackers, this spicy-sweet jam is also good with roasted or grilled meats, sandwiches, and vegetables.

4-6 red bell peppers, seeded
4-6 red chilies, seeded
  2 cups homemade cilantro or
      hot pepper red wine vinegar
      (see page 101)
  6 cups sugar
  6 ounces liquid pectin

1. In a food processor or blender, puree the two types of peppers separately until you have 1¾ cups pureed sweet peppers and ½ cup hot peppers.

2. In a large, heavy nonreactive kettle, combine the pureed peppers, vinegar, and sugar. Place over medium-high heat and cook, stirring constantly, until the sugar dissolves. Bring to a boil, continuing to stir, and cook for 4 minutes.

3. Stir in the pectin and bring to a rolling boil that can't be stirred down. Cook for 1 minute longer. Skim off any foam from the surface, then ladle the jam into hot, sterilized half-pint canning jars, leaving ¼-inch headspace. Wipe the rims and attach two-piece canning lids. Process 5 minutes in a boiling-water bath (place jars on a rack in a deep kettle and cover with water about ¼ inch above lids).

MAKES 8 HALF-PINT JARS

Herb Crabapple Jelly

Herbs blend wonderfully with apples and crabapples. If you can find cooking crabapples (the ones from the decorative trees are not the same), the jelly will have a glorious rosy color. Apples have enough natural pectin to make jelly on their own.

  2 cups apple juice
  ½ cup mint, basil thyme, lemon
      verbena, or French tarragon leaves
  ¾ cup sugar

1. Combine the juices, leaves, and sugar in a medium saucepan. Heat until sugar dissolves and mixture has jellied, about 30 minutes.

2. Pour into hot, sterilized canning jars with two-piece lids, leaving a ¼-inch headspace. Process 5 minutes in a boiling-water bath (place jars on a rack in a deep kettle and cover with water about ¼ inch above lids).

MAKES 2 HALF-PINT JARS

Chives

Allium schoenoprasum

Members of the remarkably versatile onion family, chives are native to Asia Minor. Their thin, gracefully cylindrical, deep green leaves have a mildly pungent, oniony aroma and flavor. The leaves are topped with lavender or purple ball-shaped clusters of small cloverlike flowers in late spring to early summer. Also known as Chinese chives, garlic chives *(A. tuberosum)* are a closely related species with a delicious, subtle garlic flavor. Their leaves are flat in contrast to the round leaves of regular chives, and their flowers are white and fall blooming. Chives are extremely easy to grow and can be harvested from spring to fall. Deadhead faithfully and the plant will continue to produce blossoms.

The Foolproof Herb

If you've never grown herbs before, chives are a good one for beginners. They're hardy and hard to kill, and you'll get a lot for a little work.

GROW IT. Sow seeds indoors in spring, about four seeds to an inch of surface, and cover them lightly with soil; keep at about room temperature. Once seedlings emerge, harden the plants off and transplant them to the garden in clumps of a few plants each. Space clumps about 6 inches apart. As the plants grow larger, top-dress by lightly sprinkling compost over the clumps. Chives are vigorous growers and should be divided every 3 years: lift the entire clump and separate as needed, then amend the soil with compost or well-rotted manure.

Chives are hardy and will forgive imperfect growing conditions. The variety 'Forescate' is more vigorous than the species, with longer, thicker leaves and larger flowers.

HARVEST YOUR BOUNTY. Harvest fresh green leaves continually from early spring to fall. It's best to let plants grow at least 6 inches before pruning, to ensure that growth continues. Always cut stalks at the lowest point you can reach. For garlic chives, pull up the entire plant (roots and all).

SOIL	Fertile, well drained
LIGHT	Full sun to light shade
PLANT TYPE	Perennial
HARDINESS	Zones 3–9

A Mild Onion

What can't you do with chives? Maybe they wouldn't work with chocolate, but they will enhance most any other food. They don't preserve well, though, so eat 'em fresh and often!

USES. The diced herb brings a mild onion flavor to salads, soft cheeses, eggs, potatoes, and gravies. The fresh or dried leaves can season soups and stews. Separate the petals from fresh flower heads and sprinkle them over salads. In the flower garden, chives enhance the growth of roses.

PRESERVE FOR LATER. Chives kept in a glass or vase of fresh water will stay fresh and flavorful for over a week. For longer storage, wrap the base of the bunch in a thoroughly wet paper towel, place the whole thing in a plastic bag, and lightly twist-shut the top, then store in the refrigerator drawer for up to about 3 weeks. Chives can also be dried on a paper towel for a few days or frozen for use in cooked dishes (their texture will suffer when frozen).

PART OF PLANT USED	Leaves and blossoms
CULINARY COMPANIONS	Basil, dill, oregano, rosemary, sage, thyme
USE TIP	Use it in place of scallions for a milder flavor.

CHIVE BLOSSOM VINEGAR

When your chives begin to bloom and you have to cut the blossoms to encourage new growth, put the blossoms in a large glass jar with a tight lid. Fill the jar with white vinegar and keep it in a dark place.

Whenever you cut blossoms, add them to the jar with the rest and let them all marinate until fall. When the glories of the summer garden have faded into brown twigs and brittle leaves, pull out your jar of chive vinegar and strain out the blossoms. The vinegar that remains will be as brightly pink as the blossoms once were and as redolent with their fresh summer aroma.

Bottle the vinegar in pretty jars for gifts, putting a few dried pink chive blossoms in each one.

Accenting Sauces with Herbs

Herbs are a healthy way to bring flavor to sauces for meat, seafood, and poultry without adding sodium. The sauce ensures that the protein is kept moist, and the herbs enhance the aroma and flavor of the sauce, making it all the more palatable. Red wines are a good base for red meats; white wines for fish and poultry; and butter for everything! There are some traditional herb-meat combinations, like thyme with beef and dill with fish, but let your taste buds be your guide and experiment.

Chive and Dill Sauce for Fish

A member of the onion family, chives work well both for mild onion flavor and as a garnish. Use the feathery leaves of dill in this sauce and garnish each plate with a handsome head of dill in bloom.

  4 tablespoons unsalted butter
  2 tablespoons snipped fresh chives
  1 teaspoon lemon juice
  ½ teaspoon dry mustard
  2 teaspoons finely snipped fresh dill
  4 fish fillets

1. Over low heat, melt the butter in a medium skillet, add the chives, and cook for about 2 minutes.

2. Blend in the lemon juice, mustard, and dill.

3. Bake, broil, or poach the fish fillets. Pour the sauce over the fillets and serve.

SERVES 4

Filet of Beef with Thyme and Madeira Sauce

The juicy tenderness of filet mignon is perfectly paired with a very dry, delicate Madeira and the thyme. Among the best thymes for cooking are those labeled English and French.

3 tablespoons black peppercorns

2 teaspoons fresh rosemary leaves

6 cloves garlic

1 tablespoon salt

3 tablespoons olive oil

One 2½- to 3-pound filet mignon, trimmed

Ten 4-inch sprigs fresh thyme

½ pound carrots, chopped

1 stalk celery, cut in ½-inch slices

¼ cup chopped shallots

1 cup dry Madeira

½ cup dry red wine

1 tablespoon sherry vinegar

6 ounces beef stock or canned beef broth

1. Grind the peppercorns and rosemary in a blender until they are mostly pulverized; a few small chunks are fine. Add the garlic and salt, and process. Add 2 tablespoons of the oil in a thin, slow stream, blending until the mixture is a spreadable paste. Rub the mixture all over the filet, then let the meat stand for 2 hours at room temperature.

2. Preheat the oven to 350°F. Scrape most of the spice rub off the filet, reserving ½ teaspoon. Heat the remaining 1 tablespoon oil in an ovenproof skillet over high heat and brown the filet mignon on all sides. Because of the pepper in the rub, the crust that forms will be almost black. When the meat is seared on all sides, put the skillet in the oven and cook for 25 to 30 minutes, depending on the desired doneness.

3. Remove the filet from the oven and wrap loosely in foil. Scrape any burned pieces out of the skillet and add the thyme, carrots, celery, and shallots. Cook over medium heat, stirring, for 3 minutes, or until the thyme is fragrant. Stir in the Madeira, wine, vinegar, and stock. Reduce the liquid to 1 cup. Add any juice that has accumulated in the foil, and season with the reserved pepper rub. Strain the sauce and serve immediately with the sliced filet.

SERVES 8

Cilantro & Coriander

Coriandrum sativum

When Mexican foods became popular in the United States, cooks became more familiar with the plant that had been called fresh coriander or Chinese parsley. Today, coriander generally refers to the seeds, while cilantro refers to the fresh leaves. The leaves lose their flavor and aroma when dried or frozen, so they are used almost exclusively fresh. In addition to its popularity in Mexican cooking, cilantro is a defining flavor in the cooking of Southeast Asia and is used extensively in Middle Eastern and Chinese cooking. Sweet, fragrant coriander seeds are used in curries and in many Middle Eastern dishes. They are also commonly used in sausage and are one of the spices in mixed pickling spice.

Green Leaves for Spring and Summer Seeds

Are you planting cilantro for its foliage or to harvest seeds? This decision will dictate when and where to plant.

GROW IT. Direct-sow seeds outdoors after the danger of frost has passed, and lightly cover with soil. Thin to 4 to 6 inches apart. Cultivate to reduce competition from weeds. If planting for coriander seed, plant seeds in summer in full sun, keep plants on the dry side, and don't feed them. If planting for foliage, plant in spring or fall in part shade and keep watered and fed. Pinching flower stems slows down bolting.

To keep a steady supply of green cilantro, try planting a new batch of seed every 2 or 3 weeks. Cilantro is a good companion plant for anise but not for fennel.

HARVEST YOUR BOUNTY. Harvest the leaves anytime; harvest the seeds when the plants have turned brown but before the seeds scatter. The seeds will smell deliciously spicy.

SOIL	Fertile, well drained
LIGHT	Full sun to light shade
PLANT TYPE	Annual

Coriander seeds

A Starring Role in Eastern Cooking

For those who love cilantro, they can't get enough of it. It is one of the most ubiquitous herbs in Middle and Far Eastern cooking.

USES. The flavorful dried seeds taste of citrus and can be chewed to relieve upset stomachs. The ground seeds are used in seasoning bakery products, eggs, soft cheeses, and sauces, as well as in pickling recipes and salad dressings. The fresh leaves have a strong flavor reminiscent of sage and lemon combined. They are used extensively in the cuisines of the Middle and Far East.

PRESERVE FOR LATER. The flavor of cilantro leaves disappears when dried or frozen, so to preserve the leaves it's best to make cilantro butter, oil, or vinegar (white wine vinegar is best). Dry the seeds thoroughly before using; the aroma gets stronger and more pleasing as they dry.

PART OF PLANT USED	Leaves and seeds
CULINARY COMPANIONS	Cumin, garlic, ginger
USE TIP	Toast coriander before adding to dishes; add cilantro leaves just before serving.

COOKING WITH CORIANDER

Here are some ways to incorporate coriander into your cooking:

- Combine ground coriander with minced peeled fresh ginger and butter, and stuff the mixture under the skin of a chicken before broiling. Or add it to stuffings.
- Mix ground coriander with equal parts freshly ground black pepper and ground ginger and a little salt; rub into a pork tenderloin, let sit 15 minutes, brown quickly in just a little oil, roast at 400°F for 20 minutes, turning a time or two.
- Mix with chopped green onions and use to season cooked peas.
- Add with a little orange zest to carrots.
- Mix into eggs before scrambling.
- Add to the spices in gingerbread or spice cookies.

Making Salsas

Cilantro is an integral part of most salsas. Sure, there are variations on the traditional (peach salsa, anyone?), but nothing says summer better than a salsa made with fresh tomatoes, cilantro, and garlic. You can eat your salsa right away, but it's often best to let the flavors blend for a few hours before serving.

Fresh Tomato Salsa

This salsa is not just for chips; try it over scrambled eggs. Lovers of spicy salsa should add a dash of bottled hot sauce before serving.

- ⅔ pound tomatoes, peeled, seeded, and finely chopped
- ½ cup finely chopped green bell pepper
- ¼ cup finely chopped onion
- 1 jalapeño chile, seeded and finely chopped
- 1 clove garlic, finely chopped
- 2 teaspoons minced fresh cilantro leaves
- 1 teaspoon olive oil
- ½ teaspoon salt

Combine all the ingredients in a large bowl. Use immediately, or cover and refrigerate for up to 3 days.

MAKES ABOUT 1½ CUPS

Red Onion, Mango, and Chile Salsa

This version of the popular Mexican–Latin American salsa is full of intense, contrasting flavors. It is an excellent accompaniment to grilled fish or steak, as well as stews, steamed vegetables, rice, and beans. Use whatever combination of fresh chilies your palate prefers.

1½ cups chopped mango
1½ cups chopped papaya
1 cup finely chopped red bell pepper
1 cup chopped fresh cilantro leaves
1½ cups finely chopped red onion
½ cup finely chopped fresh chilies
6 tablespoons lime juice
2½ tablespoons red wine vinegar
2 tablespoons lemon juice
2 tablespoons olive oil
2 teaspoons ground cumin
1 teaspoon salt
1 teaspoon freshly ground black pepper

Place all the ingredients in a large bowl and mix well. Cover and let stand 2 hours, allowing the flavors to blend.

MAKES 6 CUPS

Summer Vegetable Salsa

Serve over pasta or with grilled meats, fish, or poultry.

3 cups diced tomatoes
1 cup peeled, seeded, and finely chopped cucumber
½ cup cooked corn kernels
½ cup thinly sliced green onion
½ cup seeded, diced green bell pepper
¼ cup diced celery
½ cup homemade cilantro red wine vinegar (see page 101)
¼ cup extra-virgin olive oil
¼ cup minced fresh cilantro
2 tablespoons grated horseradish (fresh or preserved in vinegar)
2 tablespoons minced fresh parsley
2 cloves garlic, minced
1 small hot green chile, seeded and minced
1 teaspoon salt
½ teaspoon ground cumin
½ teaspoon freshly ground black pepper

Combine all the ingredients in a large non-reactive bowl. Serve chilled.

MAKES 4 CUPS

Dill

Anethum graveolens

Dill's common name comes from a Norse word meaning "to lull" and refers to the fact that the herb was once used to induce sleep. Similar to fennel, with highly dissected, deeply lobed leaves that have a soft, fernlike texture and pleasing aroma, dill has a tall, single, hollow stem crowned with pale yellow flowers borne in flattened umbels in summer, followed by brown, distinctively aromatic seeds. A popular culinary herb, dill is distinctive and flavorful at every stage. The young leaves have a buttery green flavor with citrus notes, while the seeds are more strongly flavored, resembling caraway. Even the yellow blooms can be used as you would use the leaves.

A Cabbage Lover

Frilly dill looks beautiful in the garden, and it loves to be planted near cabbage.

GROW IT. Dill dislikes being transplanted. Direct-sow in shallow trenches after danger of frost has passed. When seedlings are a few inches high, thin to about 8 inches apart. Keep soil moist until plants are well established. Dill makes an excellent companion to cabbage but should not be planted near carrots or fennel, with which it can hybridize. Because it grows to be up to 3½ feet tall, it's best to put it at the back of your herb garden so it won't overshadow your other plants. If you are planting dill in containers, make sure they are deep enough.

HARVEST YOUR BOUNTY. Harvest the leaves as needed; use them fresh or freeze them for later. The seeds become ripe a few weeks after the plants blossom. Cut the stems when the uppermost seeds are tan in color but before the lower seeds ripen.

SOIL	Fertile, well drained
LIGHT	Full sun
PLANT TYPE	Annual

CARMINATIVE SEEDS

Carminatives are a class of remedies used in medicine for the relief of gastric and intestinal discomfort caused by the collection of gases formed during imperfect digestion. The seeds of dill, fennel, caraway, coriander, and cumin are often brewed, separately or together, to make a tummy-soothing tea for infants and adults. Just lightly crush 1 teaspoon seeds, combine with 1 cup boiling water, and let steep for 10 minutes. Sweeten to taste with honey.

For Pickles and So Much More

Dill is a key ingredient in most traditional pickles, but its range goes far beyond those briny cucumber delights.

USES. Once highly regarded as a medicinal herb that was said to cure everything from flatulence to hiccups, dill is still used to calm digestive disorders and relieve cramps. Fresh dill is used to flavor vinegars and pickles and to add a unique taste to salads. The fresh or dried leaves and seeds are also used in seafood recipes, salad dressings, sauces, stews, butter and cheese spreads, and egg dishes; on grilled and steamed vegetables; and as a seasoning for lamb, pork, and poultry.

PRESERVE FOR LATER. Hang stems upside down in a hot, dry place with the heads just inside a brown paper bag. Or try drying dill in a microwave oven: Spread in a single layer on paper towels, and microwave on high for 3 minutes. Remove and discard the hard stems and crumble the leaves with your fingers. Store both crushed leaves and seeds in an airtight container. You can also freeze dill or preserve it in butter or vinegar.

PART OF PLANT USED	Leaves and seeds
CULINARY COMPANIONS	Cabbage, cucumbers, potatoes
USE TIP	Use to flavor pickles, salads, butters, and fish.

Making Pickles

When you say "dill," most people think immediately of cucumber pickles. But other vegetables also work well pickled with dill. In the South, for instance, you'll find okra dill pickles, which are pretty darn good, as are those made from Jerusalem artichokes. Carrots have been made into dill pickles, and so have small green tomatoes. You can also pickle with other spices, such as mints, summer savory, oregano, basil, fennel, caraway seeds, and tarragon.

NOTE: Because the flavor of most pickles is intensified after sitting for at least a couple of weeks, be sure to properly seal your jars. For in-depth pickling instructions, see Pickles and Relishes, by Andrea Chesman (Storey Publishing, 2002).

Country Dill Pickles

These resemble the country store pickles our grandparents enjoyed, the ones they fished out of big barrels or crocks.

- 1 tablespoon mixed pickling spices
- 4 heads and stems of fresh dill
- 4 cloves garlic
- 4 quarts 'Kirby' pickling cucumbers
- 2 quarts vinegar
- 1 quart water
- 1 cup kosher or other coarse salt

1. Sterilize four 1-quart jars (try to find and use the widemouthed jars).

2. Divide the pickling spices among the jars. Put 1 head of dill, complete with its stem, into each jar. Peel the garlic cloves, and put 1 into each jar.

3. Scrub the cucumbers well, then place in the jars, cramming them in as best you can.

4. Put the vinegar, water, and salt in a medium, nonreactive saucepan and bring to a boil. Pour over the cucumbers, filling the jars to within ½ inch of the top. Seal.

5. Restrain yourself — try not to eat the pickles for at least a week!

MAKES 4 QUARTS

Dilly Beans

These make a remarkable little appetizer.

- 2 quarts green beans, all the same size
- 2 teaspoons salt
- 2 quarts plus 7 cups water
- 4 large sprigs fresh dill
- 1 cup cider vinegar

1. Trim the green beans. Remove any strings, if necessary. (It hardly ever is these days; the strings seem to have been bred out of most strains of green beans.)

2. Combine the salt and 2 quarts of the water in a large saucepan. Over high heat, bring to a boil and stir until the salt is dissolved. Add the beans, reduce heat to medium and cook for 5 to 7 minutes, or until tender-crisp. Drain well.

3. Meanwhile, sterilize two wide mouthed quart jars or eight half-pint ones. Pack the green beans into the jars, dividing the dill among them.

4. Combine the remaining 7 cups water with the vinegar in a medium nonreactive saucepan and bring to a full boil over high heat. Pour into the jars. Seal. Let sit for at least 2 weeks before using.

MAKES 2 QUARTS

Basil Beans

Try these with some fresh tomatoes!

4 pounds green beans, trimmed
   (about 16 cups)
5 cups white vinegar
5 cups water
¼ cup pickling salt
16 black peppercorns
8 cloves garlic
24 fresh basil leaves

1. Wash the green beans and cut into 4-inch pieces.

2. In a medium nonreactive saucepan, combine the vinegar, water, and salt. Bring to a boil.

3. Meanwhile, into each of 8 clean, hot pint jars, put 2 peppercorns, 1 garlic clove, and 3 basil leaves. Pack the jars with the beans. Cover with the boiling hot brine, leaving ½ inch headspace.

4. Seal and process for 10 minutes in a boiling-water-bath canner. Store the jars for at least 6 weeks before opening.

MAKES 8 PINTS

TIPS FOR USING HERBS IN PICKLES

- Always use fresh herbs and spices purchased or preserved especially for that season.
- Never use anything more than a year old when beginning any pickling project.
- To obtain a clear pickle brine, use whole spices and herbs only: ground spices and herbs will make the brine cloudy.
- If you are substituting ground spices for whole, use one-quarter as much.
- When adding spices and herbs, tie them in a cheesecloth bag, and unless otherwise noted in your pickling recipe, remove them when you're packing the finished product.
- Leave spices and herbs in the jar only if the recipe specifies it. Leaving them in will darken the foodstuffs and intensify the flavor.

Florence fennel

Fennel

Foeniculum vulgare

Fennel strongly resembles dill, with its tall, fat, hollow stalks. The fernlike leaves have a sweet, anise flavor and are so fine as to appear as insubstantial as mist. The pale yellow flowers grow in shallow umbels high atop the stems in summer. Florence fennel *(F. vulgare* var. *azoricum)* has an unusual, succulent, licorice-flavored, bulb-shaped stem base that is eaten raw in salads and cooked in gratins, sautés, and casseroles. Wild fennel *(F. vulgare)* produces the tastiest seeds. Bronze fennel *(F. vulgare* 'Purpureum') is the most ornamental, sporting attractive plumes of bronze-purple foliage.

Dill's Twin

Fennel looks a lot like dill, and like dill it doesn't transplant well, so sow it where you want it. The flavor, however, is more anise than dill.

GROW IT. Fennel transplants poorly. Direct-sow it in shallow holes spaced 6 inches apart in moist soil in spring. Once plants reach about 6 inches tall, let the soil dry out between waterings. For extra-tender stem bases, mound soil up around the base to blanch them. The flowers attract beneficial insects, including hoverflies. Do not plant fennel near beans, tomatoes, kohlrabi, or dill. Fennel does not grow well next to cilantro, and artemisia can inhibit flower formation.

HARVEST YOUR BOUNTY. All parts of fennel are edible, and the leaves can be gathered as soon as the plant is established and growing well. The thick bulbs at the base of the stems are eaten as a vegetable; they reach peak flavor after the flower buds have formed but before the blossoms begin to open. Collect the seeds when the seed head begins to turn from greenish yellow to brown.

SOIL	Rich, well drained
LIGHT	Full sun
PLANT TYPE	Perennial
HARDINESS	Zones (4) 5-9

The Thrifty Person's Friend

For those looking to get the most use out of their herbs, fennel is a great choice. The entire plant is used, from leaves to roots.

USES. Fresh leaves are used in salads and on fish, and the fresh stalks can be eaten like celery. Use the seeds to flavor everything from sausages, fish, and desserts to breads and vegetables.

PRESERVE FOR LATER. Let seeds fall into a paper bag. Close up the top of the bag and store it in a cool, dry place. The seeds will complete their ripening in the bag. Once they are fully ripe, store them in a jar.

PART OF PLANT USED	Entire plant
CULINARY COMPANIONS	Fish, meat, eggs
USE TIP	The flavor of the young fennel fronds is much milder and sweeter than that of older fronds.

DON'T FORGET THE ROOTS!

A plant from which roots are to be gathered (such as caraway, fennel, and parsley root) usually needs to reach a certain maturity before its valuable properties are developed, several years in some cases. Autumn is usually the best time to harvest roots. Dig or gently pull up the plant, shake off any excess dirt, and cut off part of the root, leaving enough to support the plant's continued growth; then put the plant back into the ground.

Wash the roots you've harvested in cool water, trimming off side roots. Split the roots in half lengthwise and chop so they'll dry more quickly. When they're thoroughly dry, grind the pieces to powder in a coffee grinder to release the flavor. Properly stored in dark glass jars in a dark, cool place, roots can last 2 to 3 years.

Flavoring Meat Dishes

Some herbs (particularly fennel, rosemary, sage, savory, and thyme) add another dimension to the flavor of meat. They are often used to add flavoring to prepared meats, such as sausage, as well as to flavor stews when slow-cooked with the meat.

Lamb Stew with Rosemary and Sage

Both rosemary and sage have a camphorous aspect to their flavors, which proves to be an admirable complement to lamb.

1	tablespoon canola oil
1½	pounds boneless lamb, cut into 1½-inch cubes
1	tablespoon minced fresh rosemary leaves
1	tablespoon minced fresh sage leaves
1	clove garlic, minced
2	teaspoons flour
⅓	cup red wine–herb vinegar
⅔	cup vegetable stock or canned vegetable broth
2	anchovy fillets, minced
2	tablespoons minced fresh parsley leaves

1. Heat the oil in a large skillet over medium heat. Add the lamb and cook, stirring, until the meat is browned on all sides. Add the rosemary, sage, and garlic and cook, stirring occasionally, for 3 minutes. Sprinkle with the flour, stir, and cook for 1 minute.

2. Slowly add the vinegar and stock and stir well. Cover and reduce the heat to low. Simmer for 40 minutes, or until the meat is tender.

3. Mix a little of the hot liquid with the anchovies, then stir into the stew. Simmer for 5 minutes, uncovered. Transfer to a serving dish and sprinkle with the parsley.

SERVES 4

Ziti with Fennel and Sausage

Here, fennel's sweet flavor appears twice — in the vegetable and in the seasoning for the Italian sausage. Nonetheless, the effect is subtle and delicious. The sliced Florence fennel adds a nice crunch to the dish.

2–3 tablespoons extra-virgin olive oil
 1 pound sweet or hot Italian sausage, casings removed
 2 Florence fennel bulbs, trimmed, quartered, and sliced, with 1 tablespoon fronds reserved
 1 small onion, diced
 1 28-ounce can Italian plum tomatoes with puree
 ¼ cup red wine
 2 large cloves garlic, minced
   Salt and freshly ground black pepper
 1 pound ziti or other short pasta
   Parmesan cheese, for serving

1. Heat 2 tablespoons of the oil in a large saucepan over medium-high heat. Add the sausage and sauté, crumbling and breaking the meat up with a spoon, until the meat has lost its pink color, about 8 minutes. Remove from the saucepan with a slotted spoon and drain on a plate lined with paper towels.

2. Add the additional 1 tablespoon oil to the pan if it is dry. Add the fennel and onion and sauté until the fennel is tender crisp, about 4 minutes. Return the sausage to the pan. Add the tomatoes, wine, garlic, and salt and pepper to taste. Reduce the heat to low and simmer while you prepare the pasta.

3. Bring a large pot of salted water to a boil over high heat. Add the pasta and cook until al dente. Remove about ½ cup of the pasta cooking water. Drain the pasta well.

4. Add the pasta to the sauce and mix well. Add as much of the reserved cooking water as needed if the pasta seems dry.

5. Transfer the pasta and sauce to a large serving bowl. Garnish with the reserved fennel fronds and serve, passing the Parmesan at the table.

SERVES 4–6

Adding Herbs to Salads

Don't know what to do with an herb in the kitchen? Try putting it on a salad. Healthful, flavorful, and fragrant herbs can transform virtually any salad into a gourmet delight. Flowers can be tossed in whole, but tear or cut leaves into small pieces.

Fennel, Radish, and Borage Salad with Citrus Vinaigrette

The refreshing cucumber taste of borage adds a delightful flavor to this salad. And if you feel slightly disquieted with the world, perhaps the inclusion of borage will also have its traditional effect of lifting the spirits.

½ pound Florence fennel bulbs
½ cup small, young fresh borage leaves, torn into bite-size pieces
6 ounces radishes, thinly sliced
1 tablespoon grapefruit juice
1 teaspoon white wine vinegar
½ teaspoon salt
¼ teaspoon freshly ground black pepper
2 tablespoons walnut oil
1 tablespoon canola oil

1. To prepare the fennel, first cut the top off the fennel and remove any discolored outer portions; then slice the bulb in half from top to bottom, cut out the core, and finally cut thin slices, starting at the bottom.

2. Toss the borage, radishes, and fennel together in a large serving bowl.

3. In a small bowl, combine the grapefruit juice, vinegar, salt, and pepper. Whisk in the walnut and canola oils, adding them in a thin stream. Toss and serve.

SERVES 4

Carrot Salad with Black Olives and Hyssop

A member of the mint family, hyssop has a slightly bitter flavor with an undertone of mint.

½ pound carrots, shredded (about 2½ cups)

½ cup pitted, chopped black olives

1½ tablespoons extra-virgin olive oil

2 tablespoons minced fresh hyssop leaves

1 tablespoon balsamic vinegar

1 tablespoon white wine or rice vinegar

¼ teaspoon freshly ground black pepper

Combine all the ingredients in a large bowl and toss. Cover and refrigerate for at least 2 hours to allow the flavors to blend. Garnish with fresh hyssop blossoms, if available.

SERVES 4

Fresh dill flavors this salad

Garlic

Allium sativum

Garlic is related to the onion but has a compound bulb composed of individual cloves instead of one large bulb. It has been used for both culinary and medicinal purposes for more than 5,000 years. Its origins are unclear, but certainly it has been greatly appreciated by ancient cultures in the Far East, Middle East, and Central Asia. It was brought to the Americas by Spanish, French, and Portuguese explorers. There are two types commonly grown: white, or soft neck, and pink, or stiff neck. Modern research has confirmed many of the health benefits claimed by its fans, including its antibacterial properties and its ability to lower cholesterol and reduce the risk of certain cancers.

Think Ahead

If you want garlic this summer, you'd better have planted it last fall. Garlic is one of those plants that goes in the ground at the same time you're pulling up most of the rest of your garden.

GROW IT. Garlic is planted about the time the first hard frosts occur, for harvest the following summer, or in spring to harvest a fall crop. Separate the cloves from the bulb; plant 2 inches deep and 6 inches apart in well-worked soil that is in full sun. Water thoroughly the first 3 days, then every few days. To increase the size of the bulb, remove any flower stalks as they appear.

HARVEST YOUR BOUNTY. As harvest approaches, the leaves should begin to turn brown. Dig up the cloves carefully, and dry them on a screen in a cool, shady place with good air circulation. Shake off any soil and twist off the dried leaves. Store in a dark place in an onion bag until needed.

SOIL	Rich, well drained
LIGHT	Full sun to light shade
PLANT TYPE	Perennial
HARDINESS	Zones (4) 5-9

VARIETIES OF GARLIC

There are a number of varieties of garlic. Each has its fans. The garlic you'll most commonly encounter is white or, more accurately, creamy. Here are the names and details of some of the garlics grown in this country. Many of these are descendants of garlics brought here by immigrants from Italy, Spain, France, and Germany.

NORTHERN WHITE: These bulbs are very large, easy to peel, and winter hardy. Strong flavor. The skins are white, but the cloves are tinged with red.

GERMAN RED: Cloves are light brown, with a touch of purple. Easy to peel. Stores well. Hot, spicy flavor.

ITALIAN PURPLE: White skinned, with purple stripes. Easily peeled and a good keeper. Spicy, biting flavor. The favorite of many.

SILVER SKINS: A nice garlic in every way, but grown primarily because it is soft necked, and thus suitable for braiding.

SPANISH ROJO (FORMERLY KNOWN AS MORADO DE PEDRONERA): Red-skinned cloves. Tasty; easy to peel; a good keeper. Try using some of the early, tender greens in stir-fries.

GILROY CALIFORNIA LATE GARLIC: Originally brought to California by immigrants from Italy. Large, easy-to-peel cloves. A soft-necked variety, good for braiding.

EARLY ASIAN PURPLE SKIN: Popular in China — and best grown in warm climates in the Southeast and Southwest.

Good-Tasting Medicine

From repelling vampires to fighting the common cold, garlic has many uses. It also flavors a wide variety of dishes, so be sure to plant enough for your needs.

USES. The pungent bulb was believed by the Romans to instill strength and courage, by the Egyptians to relieve headaches, and by the Chinese to lower blood pressure. Recent research shows that garlic has strong antibacterial, antiviral, and antifungal properties. It is used to treat respiratory problems and various heart ailments, and it is an indispensable ingredient in countless recipes, adding a unique zest to just about everything.

PRESERVE FOR LATER. Braiding is probably the best way to preserve garlic, since it allows air to circulate around the bulbs. Soft-neck garlic works best for braiding. Start making braids as soon as you pull the heads from the ground. Make the braids on a flat surface, adding leaves of heads as you would in a French braid. Leave a little space between heads to make it easier to remove them, and form a loop at the end for hanging. You could also preserve your garlic by making garlic salt, garlic vinegar, garlic puree, or pickled garlic.

PART OF PLANT USED	Bulbs and scapes
CULINARY COMPANIONS	Basil, tomatoes
USE TIP	Select the biggest and best bulbs for planting next year.

Making Herbal Salts

A wide variety of herbs can be preserved in salt. It works best with thin-leaved herbs such as dill, marjoram, rosemary, savory, tarragon, and thyme, but it can be satisfactory with most large-leaved herbs such as basil if you use fewer leaves and more salt.

First gather the fresh herbs and wash them carefully in cool water. Allow them to dry so that no surface moisture remains. Chop or finely cut them into very small pieces. Pour a 1-inch layer of table salt into a clean glass container. Add a layer of herb, then cover with more salt. Repeat the process, ending with a 1-inch layer of salt at the top. Use as much herb as salt. For example, if you have 1 cup of minced herbs, use 1 cup of salt to cure them. Allow the mixture to sit in layers for a few weeks. Shake thoroughly to blend the mixture before using.

Dried rosemary mixed with kosher salt

Garlic Salt

Homemade garlic salt will keep for a long time (years) without the aid of so-called anticaking ingredients found in the store-bought kind. Use fresh garlic and good salt (such as kosher salt or La Baleine sea salt from France).

6 large cloves garlic (but not elephant garlic), each encased in a thin layer of skin, which gives added flavor

1 cup coarse salt

1. Preheat the oven to 200°F.

2. Put the garlic and salt in the bowl of a food processor. Run the machine for about 30 seconds, or until the salt is starting to turn to powder and the garlic has just about disappeared.

3. Spread out the salt mixture in a large, flat baking dish and bake for about 2 hours, or until absolutely, totally, completely dry. You can tell if it's reached this state by breaking off a bit of the cake that will have formed and rubbing it between your fingers.

4. Break the salt cake up into small pieces and place them in the food processor bowl. Run the machine until all the lumps are gone and the salt is smooth.

5. Keep in a tightly closed glass jar.

MAKES ABOUT ¾ CUP

Scarborough Fair Seasoned Salt

Herbal salt blends are very useful on meats, fowl, fish, and vegetables. Here's a traditional combination. Experiment and see what else you like!

4 tablespoons parsley, dried and finely crushed

3 tablespoons sage, dried and finely crushed

2 tablespoons rosemary, dried and finely crushed

1 tablespoon thyme, dried and finely crushed

1 cup salt

Mix the herbs and salt thoroughly and store in a large-holed shaker.

MAKES ABOUT 1½ CUPS

Hyssop

Hyssopus officinalis

Hyssop is derived from a Hebrew word meaning "holy herb," because it is said to have been used to clean temples and other sacred places. From early to late summer, the strong, shrubby stems bear numerous spikes of small, purple blossoms that attract bees and butterflies from everywhere. It is primarily grown for its strongly aromatic foliage, which emits a bit of mint, a touch of camphor, and a dash of spicy warmth. A hardy perennial, new plants can be created by root division. Pruning to the first set of leaves after flowering will create a more compact plant and result in better flowering the following year. Hyssop is probably one of the secret ingredients in Chartreuse, a French liqueur.

Bury Your Nose in the Leaves

Hyssop's leaves have an almost indescribable scent that knocks you over with its strength and keeps you coming back to the garden.

GROW IT. Start seeds indoors about 2 months before planting outside, or direct-sow in spring. Cover the seeds lightly. Space or thin plants to about 1 foot apart, and clip plants often to encourage a bushy habit. Cut the plants to the ground in fall or early spring, and fertilize with a dose of fish emulsion. In the North, divide every 4 years in spring; in the South, divide every 3 years in fall. The cultivar 'Grandiflorus' has larger flowers than the straight species; 'Albus' bears abundant spikes of pure white flowers; and 'Sissinghurst' is a more compact, dwarf variety.

HARVEST YOUR BOUNTY. Harvest leaves before the flower buds open; pick the flowers individually.

SOIL	Well drained
LIGHT	Full sun to partial shade
PLANT TYPE	Shrubby perennial
HARDINESS	Zones 3–9

FRAGRANT, AIR-FRESHENING HERBS

In the old days, people kept their homes smelling fresh with "strewing herbs," herbs strewn or scattered on the floors and beds and in outhouses. The aromatic herbs masked the odors of mold and decay that were often found in dank, dark, poorly ventilated homes where animals were often housed with people. The herbs also served as pesticides to deter flies, lice, and mites. Hyssop was particularly prized for its strong fragrance. Other frequently used herbs included basil, fennel, lavender, lemon balm, marjoram, pennyroyal, sage, and winter savory. While we rarely strew herbs these days, it isn't unusual to find a decorative bowl of potpourri on a table. Potpourri is a mixture of dried, naturally fragrant plant material used to provide a gentle, natural scent.

A Substitute for Sage and Mint

Hyssop works well in any dish that can benefit from a sage-mint flavor. But use it sparingly; a little goes a long way. In large amounts, the flavor will be bitter and resinous.

USES. Use the fresh leaves and flowers sparingly to add zip to garden salads. Toss a few fresh or dried leaves into soups, stews, stuffings, or roasted meats for a warm, sage-mint flavor. Tea made from the flowers is used to control coughs and relieve congestion. An infusion of the leaves and flowers is said to calm nervous stomachs and relieve indigestion.

PRESERVE FOR LATER. Dry flowers and leaves on a screen in a well-ventilated, shaded, warm place for 2 to 5 days. Don't leave herbs hanging for more than a few days before storing them in an airtight container; the longer they hang, the less flavorful they become.

PART OF PLANT USED	Leaves and flowers
CULINARY COMPANIONS	Meat (use sparingly)
USE TIP	Sprinkle tiny amounts of the flowers over vegetables.

Lavender

Lavandula angustifolia

The region of Provence, France, is famous for its stunning fields of lavender, whose name has become synonymous with the color of flowers. Lavender is the unique flavoring in herbes de Provence, an herbal mix that also includes basil, fennel, savory, and thyme. About 20 species of lavender grow over warm hills and alpine ridges from the Mediterranean to India. The shrubby, multibranched plants are covered with a dense canopy of thin, needlelike gray-green foliage. The leaves are highly aromatic and perfume the air around them with a clean, herbal scent. The flowers are arranged in neat spikes of small lavender-blue blossoms from summer to fall.

The Queen of Aromatic Herbs

Poets write about it, farmers and gardeners make tranquil labyrinths out of it; there's nothing quite like the scent and beauty of lavender.

GROW IT. Set well-rooted plants in the garden in spring, spacing them about 16 inches apart. Cut established plants back in spring, and remove the flower stalks after the blossoms have faded. Lavender often does poorly in hot, humid weather and is sometimes grown as an annual in the South. The plants are favorites for borders and mass plantings; the most popular varieties are the 20-inch-tall 'Hidcote' and 'Munstead Dwarf', which reaches to 12 inches.

HARVEST YOUR BOUNTY. The most fragrant leaves and flowers come from unfertilized plants grown in full sun. Harvest flowers when they are dry and the buds have begun to break. Gather leaves only from well-established plants.

SOIL	Well drained
LIGHT	Full sun
PLANT TYPE	Perennial
HARDINESS	Zones 5–8

From the Bath to the Kitchen

Lavender is used to scent many bath products, but it can also be made into wonderful tea and confections.

USES. Lavender's Latin name means "to wash," a reference to its being used to scent soaps and bathwater. Added to smelling salts, cordials, and sachets that repel insects or induce a deep sleep, lavender is also used to flavor vinegar, creams, shampoos, and jellies. Lavender-scented incense creates a restful ambience, and the leaves are essential to most potpourri recipes. Tea made from the flowers is said to induce sleep, relax the body, calm depression, settle upset stomachs, and relieve tension headaches.

PRESERVE FOR LATER. Bunch and dangle leaves and flowers to dry in a warm, airy location.

PART OF PLANT USED	Leaves and flowers
CULINARY COMPANIONS	Basil, fennel, savory, thyme
USE TIP	For lavender-flavored desserts, infuse milk with lavender flowers, then use in custards, ice cream, and flans.

HOW TO MAKE A SACHET

Sachets are little cloth bags filled with fragrant herbs to perfume clothing or linens. To make the bag, cut out a strip of fabric 10½ inches by 3¼ inches. Fold in ¼ inch borders of the raw short edges toward the wrong side of the fabric and iron in place. Sew in place, then repeat, turning in the short edges ¼ inch more. Fold the fabric strip in half with right sides together. Stitch a seam on each side of the bag ¼ inch from the raw edges. Turn the bag right side out and fill it one-half to three-quarters full with lavender or a potpourri mix. Tie the bag closed with ribbon. Avoid knotting the ribbon so the filling can be replaced as needed.

Preserving Herbs in Sugar

You can preserve some of the sweeter herbs (lemon verbena and lavender work well) in sugar. The flavors blend and make lovely, subtle combinations to use instead of regular sugar in any cold food. Pack fresh herb leaves in granulated white sugar in airtight containers. Stir every day to prevent clumping. After the sugar stays dry and loose, remove the leaves before they become crumbly and use the finished "herb sugar" in iced teas or desserts. (Note: The aromatic oils bake off, so they don't work well in baked or cooked dishes.) Or, make wonderful herb candies.

Frosted Lavender Sticks

The somewhat floppy, gray-green lavender leaves and purple flowers create a soft corner in the herb garden. Sugared, the flowers are a crisply pretty nibble. You should be sure the plants have not been sprayed with herbicides or pesticides. For variety, substitute violets or rose petals for the lavender.

12 stalks fresh lavender flowers
 1 egg white, beaten until frothy
 ½ cup sugar

1. Dip the flowers in the egg white, then roll in or dust with sugar. If you are worried about eating uncooked egg whites, substitute the proper amount of hydrated, pasteurized, dried egg whites, which are available in most supermarkets.

2. Air-dry on waxed paper.

MAKES 1 DOZEN STICKS

Old-Fashioned Herbed Candies

Penny candies in the old-fashioned general store were often made with combinations of herbs, and some tasted more hot than sweet, more bitter than refreshing. Here's a recipe that can be adapted to fit everyone's taste. Herbs to try include peppermint, spearmint, orangemint, applemint, lemon verbena, and lemon catnip.

- 4 cups boiling water
- 2 cups fresh herb leaves with stems and blossoms
- 3 cups granulated sugar
- 3 cups brown sugar
- ½ tablespoon butter

1. Place leaves in a medium bowl. Pour the boiling water over the leaves and steep for 10 minutes, longer for stronger tea. Meanwhile, butter a large shallow pan.

2. Strain the leaves into a medium saucepan, add the sugars and butter to the tea, and bring it to a boil over medium heat. Continue boiling until the syrup hardens when a small amount is dropped into cold water.

3. Pour into the buttered pan and score the candy into squares before it sets, or break it up into pieces as soon as it hardens. Wrap each hardened piece in waxed paper. Store in an airtight container.

HERBAL HONEYS

Honey makes herbal teas palatable, but it is also good medicine on its own — it is very soothing for sore throats and coughs. It is also an antibacterial and is said to strengthen the immune system.

To make an herbal honey, sterilize a jar by boiling it for 10 minutes or running it through the sterilizing cycle of your dishwasher. Pack it with the herb of your choice (all of the herbs in this book are recommended). Heat enough honey to fill the jar, bringing the honey to the point where it is steaming but not boiling. Pour over the herb, seal the jar, and let it sit in a sunny window for a few days. Strain out the used herb and put a sprig of fresh herb in the jar with the flavored honey. Enjoy!

Lemon Balm

Melissa officinalis

The scientific name for lemon balm comes from the Greek word for honeybee, because honeybees come from miles around to sip the flower's sweet nectar. The plant has weak, four-sided stems that give it a floppy appearance. The small, whitish flowers appear in clusters in the leaf axils in summer. The leaves are coarsely toothed and rough to the touch, with an intoxicatingly rich lemon scent. Lemon balm is most often used for teas and beverages. The young leaves can be chopped and added to salads, salad dressings, and vegetables for a lemony flavor. Combine it with dill, parsley, or lovage to add a subtle citrus flavor to sauces.

A Bee's Beauty

Bees love lemon balm, and farmers and gardeners alike love bees. Bees are responsible for pollinating most garden crops, including all the cabbage family plants (called brassicas), beans, squashes, cucumbers, eggplant, beets, and others.

GROW IT. Sow seeds indoors about 2 months before planting time, or direct-sow in fall. Set plants (or thin them) about 2 feet apart to induce good air circulation and inhibit powdery mildew. After a plant has flowered, cut it back to encourage a second crop of leaves. In fall, cut the plant back to the ground. Deadhead using shears to prevent self-sowing and keep foliage from yellowing. The variety 'Aurea' has deep green leaves edged in gold. 'All Gold' has bright gold young leaves that mature to golden green.

HARVEST YOUR BOUNTY. Cut sprigs as you need them through the growing season. The lower leaves have a stronger aroma.

SOIL	Well drained
LIGHT	Full sun to partial shade
PLANT TYPE	Perennial
HARDINESS	Zones (4) 5–9

LOTS OF LEMON

A number of herbs produce a similar lemony perfume, perfect for adding citrus notes to teas, foods, and beauty products. Your garden conditions may favor one of these lemony companions: Lemon basil, an annual, requires full sun and rich, moist, well-drained soil. Lemongrass, a tender perennial, requires a heavy coat of mulch or an indoor winter location; it does best in full sun and rich, well-drained soil. Harvested lemongrass can be stored in the freezer. Lemon thyme, a variety of thyme, is a perennial that thrives in full sun to partial shade in hot climates with loose, well-drained gravelly soil.

A Stress Reliever

Lemon balm is said to calm the head and the stomach. Sprinkle it on salads and fish and poultry, and maybe toss in a bit extra when stressed.

USES. The fresh, rough leaves can be rubbed on the skin to repel insects or take the itch from insect bites. An infusion from fresh or dried leaves has a cool, citrus taste that induces restful sleep, lowers fevers, relieves headaches, and calms upset stomachs. The herb is also said to have antiviral and antibacterial properties. Add leaves to garden and fruit salads, and use to season fish and poultry dishes.

PRESERVE FOR LATER. Use fresh leaves or freeze them: lemon balm loses much of its flavor when dried.

PART OF PLANT USED	Leaves
CULINARY COMPANIONS	Fish, poultry, many fruits and vegetables
USE TIP	Best fresh

Making Herbal Salad Dressings

The composition of an oil-and-vinegar dressing, or vinaigrette, is essentially a vinegar and an oil, such as olive or canola, plus salt, pepper, various herbs, and other seasonings. There are no hard-and-fast rules, although traditionally there is more oil than vinegar (usually 3 parts oil to 1 part vinegar). High-quality, milder-flavored vinegars are essential. Use the best oil possible, preferably an extra-virgin olive oil or an organically grown and expeller-processed canola, safflower, or untoasted sesame oil. Experiment with more unusual oils, such as walnut, hazelnut, or avocado.

Green Dressing
This is a great dressing for salads, grilled meats, and steamed vegetables.

1 cup chopped fresh chard or sorrel
¾ cup fresh parsley
¼ cup fresh basil
½ cup extra-virgin olive oil
¼ cup sherry vinegar
½ teaspoon curry powder
1 clove garlic, minced
   Salt and freshly ground black pepper

Combine all the ingredients in a blender and process until smooth. Cover and chill for several hours before using to allow the flavors to blend. Store, tightly covered, in the refrigerator.

MAKES 1¼ CUPS

Creamy Dressing

Great for tossed green salads; use different flavored vinegars and herbs for this dressing. Double the amount of mayonnaise or use a 3-ounce package of low-fat cream cheese to turn this dressing into a dip.

⅔ cup plain nonfat yogurt or low-fat or nonfat sour cream

⅓ cup reduced-calorie mayonnaise

2 tablespoons flavored vinegar

2 tablespoons minced fresh herbs, 1 tablespoon herb seeds, or 1 tablespoon minced peeled fresh ginger or horseradish

1 teaspoon Dijon mustard

¼ teaspoon freshly ground black pepper or hot red pepper sauce

Whisk all the ingredients together in a nonreactive bowl. Let sit an hour before using to allow the flavors to blend. Store in a tightly covered jar in the refrigerator.

MAKES 1 CUP

Asian Dressing

This is a great dressing for fish, as well as simple greens.

½ cup untoasted sesame oil

¼ cup homemade ginger sherry vinegar (see page 101)

¼ cup thinly sliced green onions

¼ cup minced fresh cilantro

2 tablespoons tahini (optional)

1 tablespoon minced peeled fresh ginger

1 tablespoon soy sauce

1 teaspoon hot red pepper sauce

1 teaspoon honey

1 teaspoon ground cumin

1 clove garlic, minced

Combine all the ingredients in a blender and process until smooth. Cover and chill for several hours before using to allow the flavors to blend. Store, tightly covered, in the refrigerator.

MAKES 1 CUP

Lemon Verbena

Aloysia triphylla

Lemon verbena is a multistemmed woody shrub native to warm regions of Chile and Argentina. In the eighteenth century, the plant was brought to Europe by the Spanish and Portuguese. In Victorian times, lemon verbena's sweet-scented oil was used to create popular perfumes and colognes reputed to induce passion in anyone who smelled them. The herb has long, woody stems with highly aromatic, lance-shaped leaves. The flowers consist of small spikes of tiny white blossoms. A tender perennial, the plant, left untended, will grow about 3 feet in a season. In a frost-free garden, it can reach heights of 10 feet, so vigorous pruning is recommended.

Contain Your Herb

Lemon verbena is best grown in containers so it can be brought inside in winter and enjoyed year-round.

GROW IT. Lemon verbena can't be grown from seed, so propagate by rooting stem cuttings in summer. Grow it in a container so you can move it outdoors in summer and indoors in winter. It thrives in rich potting soil amended with compost and fertilized regularly. This vigorous plant should be tip-pruned often to keep it compact and to encourage branching. Don't overwater, especially in winter. Plants brought indoors for the winter will drop their leaves and rest for about a month before beginning to grow again.

HARVEST YOUR BOUNTY. Harvest leaves throughout the growing season.

SOIL	Rich, evenly moist
LIGHT	Full sun
PLANT TYPE	Perennial
HARDINESS	Zones 9–10

RETAIN THAT MOISTURE!

The key to keeping a cutting alive is stopping the evaporation of water from its leaves. This can be achieved by covering the plant with plastic. To make a small plastic tent, use a large, clear polyethylene bag. Fill a clean container (6 inches wide or larger) with moist propagation mix, stick the cuttings into the mix, and water. Bend two metal coat hangers into arches and place the ends into the soil. Put the bag over the pot, fastening the loose end with a twist tie. Keep the pot out of direct light so cuttings don't overheat.

A Lasting Aroma

Treat the fresh herb like basil, and store it in resealable bags in the vegetable crisper for up to 2 days. The aroma of the dried herb will last for quite some time.

USES. A popular ingredient in soaps and bath products in years past, lemon verbena has a sweet, earthy, long-lasting lemon fragrance. Tea made from the fresh or dried leaves was said to ease stomach pains and reduce fevers, and the oil has insecticidal as well as antibacterial properties. Fresh leaves were also added to stuffings or (sparingly) garden salads. Remove stiff leaves before serving.

PRESERVE FOR LATER. When dried, the leaves retain their fragrance for many years. In fact, their lemon scent lasts longer than that of any other lemony herb. Dry leaves on a screen in a cool, dark, well-ventilated spot. The flavor is also preserved through freezing.

PART OF PLANT USED	Leaves
CULINARY COMPANIONS	Chiles, cilantro, garlic, mint
USE TIP	Use fresh leaves in place of lemongrass.

OVERWINTERING

To overwinter lemon verbena, try this tip from Steven Foster, an Arkansas-based herbalist: cut them back severely, then dig up the roots and cover them with moist sand. Store in an unheated cellar for the winter.

Pairing Herbs with Fruit

Some herbs work well with fruits, like lemon verbena and apples, or lavender and peaches. Fresh lemon balm and mint taste good on a fruit salad, but mostly you'll want to cook the herb and the fruit together so that the flavors can marry. Try compotes, chutneys, tarts, and pies. Experiment and see what tickles your fancy.

Apple–Lemon Verbena Compote

A compote is fruit cooked in syrup. This tastes divine spread on a fresh, warm biscuit.

- 2 tablespoons butter
- 2 pounds cooking apples, peeled, cored, and cut into ¾-inch dice
- 2 whole cloves
- ¼ teaspoon ground allspice
- 1 tablespoon sugar
- 1 bay leaf
- ½ cup fresh lemon verbena leaves
- 1 cup apple juice
- ¼ cup lemon juice

1. In a large saucepan, melt the butter over medium-high heat until it foams, then add the apples, cloves, allspice, sugar, and bay leaf. Stirring, cook until almost dry.

2. Stir in the lemon verbena and ¼ cup of the apple juice. Mix the remaining ¾ cup apple juice and the lemon juice together in a measuring cup and set aside. Reduce the heat to low, cover, and cook for 40 minutes, adding a tablespoon of the apple–lemon juice mixture every 10 minutes, or as needed to keep the compote from drying out.

3. The compote is done when its color is light brown and the apples are halfway broken down. Serve warm or chilled.

MAKES 2 CUPS

Cranberry Chutney

Chutneys are usually hot, spicy-sweet mixtures of chopped fruits or vegetables — a combination pickle and preserve, sweet and sour. They are customary accompaniments to Indian and similar cuisines, but don't overlook them as flavorings for cold cuts and roasted meats.

6 cups fresh cranberries

2 medium navel oranges, rind grated, pith discarded, and the fruit coarsely chopped

2 cups chopped cored apples

1 cup chopped onion

1 cup raisins

1 cup chopped pecans

1 cup orange juice

1 clove garlic, minced

2 cups packed light brown sugar

½ cup homemade tarragon or hyssop vinegar (see page 101)

¼ teaspoon ground ginger

½ teaspoon ground cloves

½ teaspoon ground allspice

½ teaspoon ground cinnamon

1. Combine all the ingredients in a heavy-bottomed, nonreactive pot. Bring to a boil over medium heat, stirring constantly.

2. Reduce the heat to low and simmer for 20 minutes, stirring frequently. Pour into hot, sterilized canning jars and process 5 minutes in a boiling-water-bath canner.

MAKES 8 HALF-PINTS

SUGGESTED COMBINATIONS

If you've ever enjoyed strawberries with a sprinkle of basil and balsamic vinegar, you know that herb-fruit combinations can be sublime. Still, when it comes to flavoring fruit, most people reach for the reliable baking spices: cinnamon, nutmeg, and ginger. Here are some different combinations to consider:

- **APPLES:** anise hyssop, bee balm, lovage, mint, rosemary, sage
- **APRICOTS:** anise hyssop, basil, lemon verbena
- **CANTALOUPE:** basil, cilantro, dill
- **GRAPEFRUIT:** anise hyssop, basil, cilantro, mint, tarragon
- **ORANGES:** anise hyssop, cilantro, dill, fennel, lavender, lovage
- **PEACHES:** anise hyssop, basil, lemon verbena, mint
- **PEARS:** lavender, mint, rosemary, sage
- **PINEAPPLE:** basil, cilantro, mint
- **RHUBARB:** lavender
- **STRAWBERRIES:** basil, borage, mint

Marjoram

Origanum majorana

Marjoram is known as one of the "subtle" herbs. A square-stemmed member of the mint family (called by Greeks "the joy of the mountains"), sweet marjoram is not only an aromatic kitchen herb but also an attractive addition to the garden. The plant has compact, multibranched stems densely covered with small, sweetly fragrant green leaves, and tiny white or pink flowers in late summer. Marjoram is part of the oregano genus, which includes many similar herbs. Hardy hybrid sweet marjoram (*O. × marjoricum*) is slightly more pungent than sweet marjoram; pot marjoram (*O. onites*) has a stronger flavor than sweet marjoram; and dittany, of Crete (*O. dictamnus*), has a milder scent and furry silver leaves.

Cut Back for Long Life

Here's another herb you'll need to cut back to further its growth. Prune in late spring to encourage new growth and again in midsummer to prevent woodiness.

GROW IT. Sow the tiny seeds indoors in spring and set them in the garden after the danger of frost has passed. When flower buds appear, cut the plant back by about one-third, removing all the flower buds. New leaves will form and extend the harvest time. Lift the plants in fall before the first frost, and pot them in containers. Overwinter on a sunny windowsill.

HARVEST YOUR BOUNTY. Harvest the fresh leaves as needed. The leaves are most flavorful just before the plant blooms.

SOIL	Well drained
LIGHT	Full sun
PLANT TYPE	Tender perennial
HARDINESS	Zones 9–10

WHICH IS MARJORAM, WHICH OREGANO?

Marjoram and oregano are easily confused. Because both herbs are in the same family, plants are often mislabeled in nurseries, and the two herbs will crossbreed. How do you tell the difference? Marjoram, which may be labeled "sweet marjoram" or "knotty marjoram," will have a savory, sweet, pungent aroma without a hint of spiciness, while oregano will be peppery or spicy. The buds of sweet marjoram look like little knots, and the flowers are white to pink, while the flowers of oregano are purple-pink. Sweet marjoram is much more tender than oregano and unable to survive a frost. Both combine well with other European herbs in the wide-ranging mint family, including mint, rosemary, sage, thyme, and basil.

A Substitute for Oregano?

Not quite. Marjoram is sweet, not spicy, with citrus notes and a minty edge. Oregano is hot, bold, and easily overpowers other ingredients.

USES. The flavor of sweet marjoram resembles oregano blended with mint. Infusions of fresh or dried leaves relieve congestion and headaches, settle upset stomachs, and encourage restful sleep. Its soft flavor enhances stuffings, soups, sauces, and stews, as well as meat dishes and flavored vinegars.

PRESERVE FOR LATER. Dry leaves in the refrigerator for the best flavor. To do so, gently wash in cool water and allow moisture to evaporate, then spread on a baking sheet covered with paper towels, hang in a mesh bag, or place in an uncovered bowl and stir daily. Leaves will dry in 2 to 7 days. Dried leaves have a softer, almost faint aroma when compared to the fresh leaves.

PART OF PLANT USED	Leaves
CULINARY COMPANIONS	Basil, mint, rosemary, sage, thyme
USE TIP	Taste before using; its flavor intensifies in hot weather.

FINES HERBES

Fines herbes is a French blend of very finely chopped dried herbs. It is usually made with chervil, chives, parsley, and tarragon, but may also contain marjoram, salad burnet, savory, or watercress, depending on the preference of the herb blender. The mixture is typically used to flavor omelets and other mildly flavored dishes.

To make your own fines herbes, gather equal amounts of the fresh herbs and dry them carefully on a screen in a shady spot with good air circulation. Very finely chop the herbs and store in a clean glass jar. When cooking with fines herbes, add at the end of the cooking process for the best flavor.

Making Herbal Vinegars

Vinegars preserve the flavor and character of herbs instead of the herbs themselves. Begin with a high-quality vinegar; the type you use will depend on the herb you are preserving (red wine vinegar works well with oregano and marjoram, for instance).

Fill a sterilized glass container with the washed fresh herb. Pour in the vinegar until all of the herb is covered and seal the container (use cork, plastic, ceramic, or glass lids — never metal). Place the jar on a sunny windowsill for at least a few weeks so the warm liquid can leach the flavors from the herb more efficiently. Strain the liquid into clean, sterilized jars and label. You may also wish to toss a bit of the fresh herb into the jars.

Provençal Vinegar

Here's an easy way to add a touch of the flavors of Provence in the South of France to your food.

1 small sprig fresh thyme
1 small sprig fresh rosemary
1 small bay leaf
1 large clove garlic
1 strip orange peel, about 1 inch
    by 4 inches
2 cups white wine vinegar

1. Put the thyme, rosemary, bay leaf, garlic, and orange peel into a sterilized 1-pint bottle (or put smaller amounts in each of two 8-ounce bottles).

2. Add the vinegar. Seal.

3. Store for a month before using, giving the bottle a very gentle shake every day or two.

Rosemary Vinegar

One of the easiest ways to preserve the unique flavor of rosemary is in vinegar. Use in sauces, soups, and salads.

1 quart apple cider vinegar
2 small sprigs fresh rosemary
    (or 2 tablespoons dried)
3 chilies
2 cloves garlic
2 slices lemon
1 stick cinnamon

1. Heat the vinegar gently in a medium saucepan over low heat; do not boil. Place the ingredients in a large sterilized glass container and pour the vinegar over them. Seal the container.

2. Steep on a sunny windowsill for 2 weeks before straining and using. For gifts, add fresh stems of rosemary and label. Hint: Cork the bottle, or use waxed paper under metal lids to prevent corrosion.

SUGGESTED COMBINATIONS

Some herbs combine beautifully in vinegar. Here are some possible combinations.

- Chive flowers with lemon balm in white wine vinegar
- Dill, fennel, garlic, basil, and thyme in red wine vinegar
- Garlic, chilies, and basil in red or white wine vinegar
- Ginger, chive blossoms, and savory in rice wine vinegar
- Orange zest with lemon mint leaves in white wine vinegar
- Parsley, thyme, and basil in red wine vinegar

Mint

Mentha spp.

Mint has found a home in virtually every garden. You can choose from peppermint, spearmint, apple mint, pennyroyal, lemon mint, and ginger mint, to name a few. Spearmint is the preferred mint for most savory dishes; it is less likely to overpower than other mints, particularly peppermint. Peppermint is loaded with menthol, which gives it a bracing icy flavor and is well suited to desserts, candy, and chocolate. Pennyroyal is edible but its most popular use is as an insect repellent. All mints have square stems graced with toothed, highly aromatic leaves. In summer, the small flowers appear clustered in the leaf axils or as a spike on top of the stem.

Hold It Back!

Mint will overtake your garden if you don't take precautions, such as planting it in a container. Fortunately, the plant is easily pulled up if it does invade.

GROW IT. Propagate by transplanting the suckers that rise from the roots, spacing plants about 1 foot apart. To prevent this vigorous plant from taking over the garden, surround with a plastic or metal barrier buried about 10 inches into the ground. When stems become woody, cut them back to encourage more succulent growth. Plant mint in full sun in soil that is evenly moist. Keep manure away to discourage rust disease, and remove yellow-streaked sprigs to prevent the spread of virus. Note that species of mint interbreed easily, forming hybrids that blur distinctions between species.

HARVEST YOUR BOUNTY. Gather individual leaves as needed or cut the entire stalk just as the flower buds emerge.

SOIL	Well drained
LIGHT	Full sun to partial shade
PLANT TYPE	Perennial
HARDINESS	Zones 5-9

PROPAGATE FROM ROOT CUTTINGS

Plants that send out runners (such as mint) are easy to propagate from root cuttings. Clean your knife and cutting surface with a solution of 1 part bleach to 10 parts water. Cut a runner into sections several inches long; put the cuttings into moist, sterile grower's mix in clean containers and place them in a bright location.

Enjoy Minty Goodness

From chocolate sauce to iced tea, mint can be used to flavor many dishes. It pairs well with Mediterranean flavors, such as olive oil, capers, and garlic, so try it in savory dishes, too.

USES. Infusions of fresh or dried mint leaves are said to relieve indigestion and reduce cramps. A strong tea can be used as a skin wash, and mint is a favorite ingredient in skin creams and shampoos. Use leaves to flavor drinks, jellies, and desserts, as well as soups and sauces. It repels many insects and thus is planted with vegetables and flowers.

PRESERVE FOR LATER. Peppermint is best for drying, although the fragrances and flavors of spearmint, orange mint, and apple mint also will last for years. Dry by hanging bunches upside down in a cool, dry place. The plant should dry in 2 to 5 days. Don't leave plants hanging too long; the more time they hang, the less flavorful they become. Crumble leaves into airtight jars. The flavor of mint is also retained through freezing.

PART OF PLANT USED	Leaves
CULINARY COMPANIONS	Cilantro, fruit, lemon verbena, oregano, rosemary
USE TIP	Lamb with mint jelly is a timeless combination.

Minted Chocolate Sauce

For many people with a sweet tooth, there's no better combination than mint and chocolate. To put a little zip into traditional chocolate sauce, add a little mint. The quick way is to add a few drops of peppermint extract to the chocolate sauce. Only slightly longer to prepare is the following sauce made with fresh mint.

- ½ cup water
- ½ cup coarsely chopped fresh mint leaves
- 3 squares unsweetened chocolate
- ¾ cup sugar
- ¼ teaspoon salt
- 4½ tablespoons butter or margarine
- ½ teaspoon vanilla extract

1. Boil ¼ cup water and pour over the mint leaves in a small bowl. Let stand for 10 minutes.

2. In a small saucepan, melt the chocolate over medium heat in the remaining ¼ cup water. (Or combine and heat in the microwave oven about 2 minutes, stirring after 1 minute.)

3. Strain the mint-flavored water into a small saucepan and add the melted chocolate, sugar, and salt. Cook at medium heat, stirring, about 5 minutes, or until the sugar melts and the mixture thickens.

4. Stir in the butter and vanilla, and continue heating until the butter melts. Serve hot or cold.

MAKES 1¼ CUPS

Oregano

Origanum vulgare

The word *oregano* is of Greek origin and translates as "joy of the mountains." *Origanum vulgare* subsp. *hirtum,* or common oregano, grows wild as a perennial in the mountains of Greece. It has small white flowers, can reach as tall as 2 feet, and forms dense clumps. Varieties include dark oregano (*O. vulgare* var.), which grows to 2 feet tall and has a full flavor; compact oregano (*O. vulgare* 'Compactum Nanum'), a ground cover that only grows 2 to 3 inches high; and golden creeping oregano (*O. vulgare* 'Aureum'), which grows to a height of 6 inches and has a mild flavor.

A Mediterranean Powerhouse

Oregano grows best in conditions that mimic its native Mediterranean habitat. It loves full sun and well-drained soil. In the right situation, oregano can become aggressive and invasive.

GROW IT. Seed directly into the soil in full sun after ground has thoroughly warmed. Scatter seeds thinly and gently tamp into soil. Cultivated oregano does best in light loam with a neutral to slightly alkaline pH. In soil that tends to be acidic, work in a sprinkling of wood ashes or dolomitic limestone.

If starting seeds indoors, harden off seedlings for about a week when they have at least two true leaves. Grow in full sun.

HARVEST YOUR BOUNTY. Cut back plants hard once or twice a summer, cutting to the base just before they flower.

SOIL	Average, well drained, limy
LIGHT	Full sun
PLANT TYPE	Perennial
HARDINESS	Zones 5–9

HARVESTING HINTS

The best time to harvest oregano is when flower buds appear — about 60 days after growth begins in spring. Prune to within 6 inches of the ground, leaving some leaves. If the plant has become woody, prune the plant back to half or three-quarters of its new growth. You may be able to harvest again, but not closer than 45 days from the first expected hard freeze.

Pizza Pie, Please

Perhaps its most famous use is to flavor tomato sauces on pizzas and pastas, but oregano works well in creamy dishes, too.

USES. Oregano is often used in cooking to flavor tomato sauces on pasta and pizza. Fresh oregano leaves also go well with cream sauces, eggs, and cheese.

PRESERVE FOR LATER. Oregano can be kept in the refrigerator for a few days when stored, unwashed, in a resealable bag. For longer storage, dry the oregano by tying cut stems together and hanging them upside down in a cool, dry, dark place or in a paper bag for about 2 weeks. Alternatively, you can lay the cut stems on a cookie sheet and keep them in a barely warm oven for half a day. You can also preserve the leaves in salt or freeze them in tomato juice or water.

PART OF PLANT USED	Leaves
CULINARY COMPANIONS	Rosemary, sage, thyme
USE TIP	Oregano's bold flavor should be paired with bold ingredients, such as tomatoes, olives, lemon, and garlic.

TRAVEL THE GLOBE WITH THE FLAVOR OF HERBS

The judicious use of herbs can evoke the flavors of different cuisines. The scents of basil, garlic, rosemary, and sage evoke Italy, especially when used with olive oil and anchovies. Combine basil, fennel, lavender, savory, and thyme, and you have a flavor that is unique to Provence. A dish scented with tarragon is likely to evoke many parts of France. Mexican foods are often redolent of cilantro as well as chilies. Lemon and parsley are a favorite combination in the Middle East, as is coriander seed and garlic, while garlic, cumin, and mint combine in the cooking of Egypt and northeast Africa. Sour cream combined with dill or caraway speaks of northern or eastern Europe. In Vietnam, basil, mint, and cilantro is a typical combination.

The Ultimate Pizza

Using both fresh and dried oregano gives this pizza an extra dimension.

THE CRUST
- 1 package active dry yeast
- 1 cup warm water
- 1 cup unbleached white bread flour
- 1 cup whole wheat bread flour
- 1 tablespoon corn meal
- 1 tablespoon wheat germ
- 1 teaspoon salt
- 1 teaspoon dried oregano
- 1 teaspoon sugar
- 1 teaspoon olive oil

THE SAUCE
- 1 (10¾ ounce) can tomato puree
- 2 cloves garlic, pressed
- 1 tablespoon minced fresh oregano
- 1 tablespoon Parmesan

- olive oil
- cheese of your choice
- toppings of your choice

1. Dissolve the yeast in the warm water and beat in the remaining crust ingredients.

2. When the dough forms a ball, turn it out onto a floured board and knead a few minutes until smooth and shiny.

3. Put the kneaded dough into a buttered bowl, cover with plastic wrap, and let rise in a warm place until doubled.

4. Preheat the oven to 425°F. To finish the crust, deflate the dough, let it rest for a few minutes, roll out into a circle about 16 inches in diameter or roll into a rectangle to fit a cookie sheet.

5. Place the dough on a pan sprayed with no-stick vegetable cooking spray. Place on the lower rack in the oven for about 5 minutes. The dough should be baked through, but not browned.

6. Remove from the oven and cool. You can either freeze the crust or proceed with the recipe.

7. To make the sauce, combine all the ingredients listed above.

8. Brush the partially cooked pizza dough with olive oil and spread the sauce evenly over it. Add cheese and toppings.

9. Place the pan on the bottom rack in a 450°F oven. Bake about 15 minutes, depending on your oven.

MAKES ONE 11- x 16-INCH PIZZA

Parsley

Petroselinum crispum

Parsley is the middle child of the herb garden: always there but never fully appreciated. Three types are commonly grown: curly parsley (*P. crispum*) has dark green, curled leaves; flat leaf parsley (*P. crispum* var. *neapolitanum*) has dark green, strongly flavored, flat leaves; and parsley root (*P. crispum* var. *tuberosum*) produces a fleshy, edible root. The most appealing aspect of parsley is that it blends well with almost any flavor. Because flat leaf parsley is more strongly flavored than curly parsley, it is more commonly cooked with, whereas curly parsley is more commonly used as a garnish. Parsley root looks like parsnip and can be used interchangeably with parsnips, though the flavor is quite different.

For the Patient Gardener

If it's been a couple of weeks since you sowed your parsley seeds and you still don't see any seedlings, don't despair — they'll come up, but they'll take more time.

GROW IT. Sow seeds outdoors in spring when soil temperatures reach about 50°F. Cover with a light layer of soil. Germination is slow — it can be more than a month before seedlings appear. You can speed up germination, however, by soaking seeds in warm water for 24 hours before sowing. Thin plants to 8 inches apart, and remove flower shoots and yellowing leaves as they appear. Fertilize with an organic fertilizer or mulch lightly with compost or well-rotted manure. For your winter windowsill garden, sow seeds in a 4-inch pot and place on a sunny sill. Do not overwater. One of the most popular varieties is 'Moss Curled', with its tightly rolled, compact leaves and excellent, zesty flavor.

HARVEST YOUR BOUNTY. Harvest the leaves anytime they are needed.

SOIL	Rich, evenly moist, well drained
LIGHT	Full sun to partial shade
PLANT TYPE	Biennial

THE RIGHT CONTAINER MATERIAL

A great many herbs seem to enjoy growing in containers. Pots come in a variety of styles and colors. The choice of containers is determined by the priorities of the grower. If you need portability but cannot lift heavy clay pots, then plastic is the obvious choice for you. If you grow your plants in small pots on the windowsill and want the healthiest herbs all winter long, then clay is best. In general clay pots grow better, healthier plants and are more decorative; plastic pots are less expensive and weigh less.

The Flavor Police

Used to mask bad breath and harmonize different flavors, parsley is more than just decoration.

USES. Parsley is used mainly as a culinary herb. It is especially useful for toning down strong flavors, such as garlic, without covering it up. Because it blends well with other flavors, it can be added to almost any savory dish, especially fish, poultry, and vegetables. As a breath freshener, just chew on a fresh sprig. Parsley is also a green that works well in a salad, such as tabbouleh, and it makes a lovely garnish.

PRESERVE FOR LATER. Dry the leaves in the refrigerator: first wash them in cool water and let air-dry, then spread on a baking sheet covered with paper towels, hang in a mesh bag, or store in an uncovered bowl and stir daily. Leaves should take 2 to 7 days to dry in the fridge. Store in airtight containers. The flavor is also retained through freezing.

PART OF PLANT USED	Leaves and roots
CULINARY COMPANIONS	Other herbs, meats, vegetables
USE TIP	Strip the leaves from the coarse stems before chopping.

Making Herbal Breads

Making bread is addictive. The satisfaction is enormous, not only from the actual achievement but from the accolades that envelop you as people bite into hot muffins, beautiful biscuits, or a tall loaf of herb bread. And herbs find themselves right at home in breads. Aromatic in the kitchen and tasty on the tongue, they add a very pleasing dimension to your baked goods.

Bread Bouquet Garni

If you happen to be missing one of the herbs called for below, substitute a favorite or double one of those listed. This is one for the bread machine and produces a large loaf. If you don't have a bread machine, you can certainly knead this combination of herbs into your favorite white or sourdough bread.

- ¼ cup wheat bran
- ¼ cup rolled oats
- 2½ cups unbleached all-purpose bread flour
- 2 tablespoons powdered buttermilk
- 1 cup plus 2 tablespoons water
- 1 egg
- 2 tablespoons butter
- ½ teaspoon salt
- ½ teaspoon brown sugar
- 1 teaspoon minced fresh marjoram
- 1 teaspoon minced fresh thyme
- 1 teaspoon minced fresh rosemary
- 1 teaspoon minced fresh parsley
- 1 teaspoon freshly ground black pepper
  Slightly less than 1 packet active dry yeast (2½ teaspoons)

1. Combine the wheat bran, rolled oats, bread flour, and buttermilk in a large bowl.

2. Place the ingredients in your bread machine in the order prescribed by the instruction book and let the machine do the work for you.

MAKES 1 LARGE LOAF

Thyme and Cheese Biscuits

Wheat, herbs, and cheese cause a major personality change in old-fashioned baking powder biscuits. Other herbs can be substituted for the ones here.

- ½ cup whole wheat flour
- 1½ cups unbleached all-purpose flour
- 1 tablespoon baking powder
- 1 teaspoon minced fresh thyme
- ½ teaspoon minced fresh parsley
- ½ teaspoon minced fresh rosemary
- ½ cup shredded Monterey Jack cheese
- 5 tablespoons chilled butter
- ½ cup milk, or more as needed

1. Preheat the oven to 450°F. Grease a cookie sheet and set aside. Using a fork, mix the flours, baking powder, herbs, and cheese in a large mixing bowl. Cut in the butter until the mixture is crumbly.

2. Add the milk and stir until the ingredients hold together. Add more milk if needed.

3. Drop large spoonfuls of the dough on the cookie sheet at least 1 inch apart. Bake 10 to 12 minutes, or until a toothpick inserted in the center comes out clean.

MAKES 1 DOZEN BISCUITS

TIPS FOR MAKING HERBAL BREADS

Here are a few tips for when you are making breads with herbs.

- Use fresh herbs whenever the recipe says "dried." Try twice as much at first and then tone it down — or up — the second time around to suit your own palate.
- Always wash store-bought herbs. If you're going to mince them anyway, squeeze them inside a paper towel. It's hard to chop wet herbs finely.
- For breads, mince the herbs very finely. You're looking for taste, not texture.
- Substitute French tarragon for basil, rosemary for savory, thyme for oregano, and see what you think. Pairing them is like marriage: sometimes it works, sometimes it doesn't.
- Get rid of those tough stems on the fresh herbs. Sometimes you can just pull the stem through your thumb and forefinger, down from the top. Or scrape the leaves off with a knife on a board.

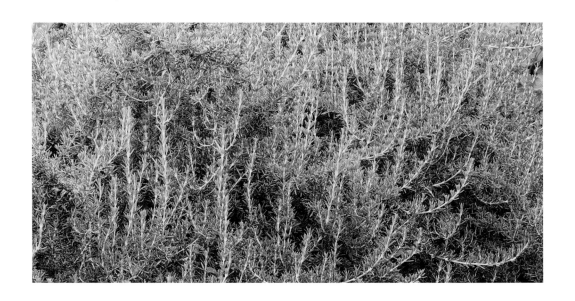

Rosemary

Rosmarinus officinalis

A native of the Mediterranean region, rosemary is said to have gotten its name because the Virgin Mary hung her cloak on it when the Holy Family fled from Herod's soldiers to the safety of Egypt. Because of its associations with constancy and remembrance, its leaves have long been used in bridal bouquets and crowns. Rosemary is an erect, evergreen shrub with thin, needle-like, dark green leaves that are strongly aromatic and penetrating but pleasantly relaxing. The plant flowers from winter through spring, bearing clusters of small white, pink, or lavender blossoms. There are many varieties, with a range of flower and foliage colors.

Water Carefully

Rosemary is picky when it comes to watering, so follow instructions carefully.

GROW IT. Propagate by rooting cuttings or by stem layering. Transplant into well-worked soil after the danger of frost has passed. Prune plants after the flowers have faded. In spring, remove dead or broken stems. Rosemary may not overwinter well when the weather is wet and cold for prolonged periods. In northern areas, it is often grown as a container plant; use a fertile, well-drained potting mix and mist frequently. Rosemary is sensitive to both underwatering and overwatering; you should water only after the soil has dried but before it *completely* dries out. Control powdery mildew by misting the leaves with cool chamomile tea.

HARVEST YOUR BOUNTY. Collect the leaves and flowers by snipping 4- to 6-inch sprigs from healthy plants. The most aromatic leaves are collected from plants just as they come into flower. Taper off your harvest in the fall, when no more than a third of your bush should be taken.

SOIL	Well drained
LIGHT	Full sun
PLANT TYPE	Tender perennial
HARDINESS	Zones (7) 8-10

MAKING MORE ROSEMARY

Rosemary is easily propagated from stem cuttings. To take a stem cutting, begin with a section of healthy stem that has been growing steadily for the past month or two. Remove the cutting with pruning shears scrubbed with a solution of 1 part bleach to 10 parts water — make a slanting cut just below the lowest set of leaves. Remove the leaves on the lower portion of the cutting, leaving only naked stem on that part. Make a hole in moist potting mix, insert the leafless base of the cutting, and press the soil firmly around it. Cover the container with clear plastic, propped up above the herb foliage. The cutting is ready to transplant when it starts to grow, or when you tug on it gently and it has enough roots to resist.

Rosemary Is for Remembrance

For many people, the smell of rosemary is comforting, conjuring memories of stews on cold winter days or potatoes roasting in the oven. The aroma is sure to bring people to the table.

USES. The fresh or dried leaves season sauces, stews, soups, and meat dishes. Use it in a bouquet garni with chicken, meat, vegetable, and tomato dishes — pull the leathery sprigs out before serving. Hot infusions are said to relieve migraine headaches and to relax the body. The herb is also used in lotions and ointments to ease muscle aches and joint pain.

PRESERVE FOR LATER. Sprigs can be gathered into bunches and hung upside down in a cool, shady place or placed in freezer bags and frozen. Kept in a clean terry towel, rosemary will stay fresh in the refrigerator for as long as 2 weeks, and the flavor is also preserved through freezing.

PART OF PLANT USED	Leaves
CULINARY COMPANIONS	Grilled and roasted meats (especially lamb), onions
USE TIP	Add freely to steaming water and marinades to add background flavor.

TIPS FOR COOKING WITH ROSEMARY

- Use rosemary to transform cauliflower into company fare.
- Cream chopped fresh rosemary into softened butter or cream cheese for a treat on hot bread.
- Garnish orange slices with rosemary.
- Try rosemary on spinach, eggplant, peas, or squash.
- Serve the flowers as an attractive edible garnish.
- Skewer shish kebabs on 12-inch lengths of rosemary.
- Enhance a variety of Mediterranean dishes with just a pinch of rosemary.
- Use several sprigs of rosemary, tied together, as a flavor-enhancing basting brush for sauces.
- Add a few leaves to any marinade.
- Try using rosemary in your fruit salad — you'll be amazed!

Making Herb Butters

Many herbs — cilantro and dill, for instance — make delicious herb butters. The simplest way is to soften unsalted butter and combine it with chopped herb and lemon juice. The proportions: 4 parts butter, 2 parts herb, ½ part lemon juice. This freezes quite nicely and will give you a touch of the herb flavor whenever you need it.

Roasted Bell Pepper and Cilantro Butter

For a different spread on crackers — perhaps even crackers you've made yourself — try this pretty butter.

4   tablespoons butter, softened
½   cup roasted red bell peppers
2   teaspoons hot mustard
1   tablespoon chopped fresh cilantro
    Salt and freshly ground black pepper

1. In a food processor or blender, cream the butter and gradually add the peppers through the top while it is running.

2. When the butter is rosy red, stop the machine and scrape the sides. Add the mustard and cilantro, process until mixed, and season with salt and pepper to taste.

3. Serve at room temperature.

MAKES ½ CUP

BEST BUTTERS

Here are some great combinations for you to mix and match in butter.

FULL-FLAVORED BUTTERS FOR LAMB OR BEANS: Rosemary or winter savory

GRILLED MEAT BLEND: Combine garlic, thyme, and sweet marjoram (baste on grilling meats)

CHICKEN OR FISH BUTTERS: Combine fennel or tarragon with dill

ALL-PURPOSE BUTTER: Parsley, marjoram, thyme, basil, and a bit of garlic

JUST-THE-BASICS BUTTER: Chives and dill

Béarnaise Butter

If you want the flavor of béarnaise sauce but don't want to use eggs, béarnaise butter is a good solution. Béarnaise is especially good with steak (or hamburgers) or broiled chicken. This can be made days ahead and kept in the refrigerator until shortly before it's needed.

1 tablespoon water

2 teaspoons vinegar (any kind except one with color, such as red wine vinegar)

1 tablespoon minced shallot

1 tablespoon minced fresh French tarragon or 1 teaspoon dry
  Pinch of cayenne pepper or 3 drops Tabasco or other hot sauce

4 tablespoons butter at room temperature

1. Combine the water, vinegar, shallot, and half of the tarragon in a very small saucepan. Boil together for 1 minute. (The moisture will be almost gone.)

2. Add the remaining tarragon and the cayenne.

3. Cream the butter in a food processor, if possible, or mash well with a fork. Gradually add the liquid mixture.

4. Let stand for at least 30 minutes to give the flavor a chance to develop. Serve at room temperature.

MAKES ABOUT ½ CUP

Dill-flavored butter

Sage

Salvia officinalis

The ancients believed that those who used sage would acquire wisdom and achieve immortality. Garden sage is native to the Mediterranean and northern Africa, where it grows into a woody, semi-erect, 3-foot-tall shrub. The evergreen leaves exude a pungent, spicy, slightly sweet scent. Other species include pineapple sage (*S. elegans*), with its bright red, tubular flowers and pineapple-scented leaves, and Spanish sage (*S. lavandulifolia*), which has narrow, gray-green leaves with the aroma of lavender and spice. Some excellent cultivars include 'Kew Gold', with bright yellow leaves; 'Icterina', with green leaves edged in gold; and 'Purpurea', a vigorous plant that bears large, richly aromatic leaves tinged with violet.

Sage Advice: Take a Cutting

If you don't have much experience growing plants, find a friend who has a sage plant and ask to have a division of hers.

GROW IT. Propagate from cuttings taken in early fall or divide older, established plants. Sage can be grown from seeds, but it takes at least 2 years to produce a useful specimen. Plant in well-worked soil and mulch with compost or well-rotted manure. Sage does not grow well when winters are wet or springs are moist and cool. In late fall, mound dry mulch over the plants to help them overwinter. Cut back old stems in spring to encourage strong new growth to emerge. Divide every couple of years to rejuvenate plants.

HARVEST YOUR BOUNTY. Harvest sage by plucking individual leaves or snip whole sprigs above pairs of leaves. The woody stems can be used as skewers for the grill. If your variety flowers, harvest the blooms to sprinkle on salads and pasta.

SOIL	Well drained
LIGHT	Full sun to partial shade
PLANT TYPE	Perennial
HARDINESS	Zones (4) 5–8

HERBS THAT CAN TAKE THE HEAT

Many herbs, such as basil and cilantro, don't stand up well to heat. These delicate leaves are best added just as a dish is removed from the heat. Not so with rosemary, sage, and thyme. These are assertive herbs with coarsely textured leaves that stand up well to the heat of the barbecue or the long, slow roast. Indeed, sage is closely associated with the Thanksgiving turkey (often in combination with thyme). Commercial poultry seasoning mix usually contains sage, thyme, celery salt, and savory. Rosemary is often used with roast lamb and pork, whereas thyme is frequently used to season beef stews and hearty winter soups.

Part of the Perfect Trio

Along with rosemary and thyme, sage makes a wonderful seasoning for meats, stews, and soups.

USES. The freshly gathered leaves of garden sage make a wonderful addition to omelets, breads, vegetables, meats, sauces, stuffings, and soups. Try rubbing a fresh leaf on a pork chop before grilling it. Leaves can also be blended with butter or soft cheese to make aromatic spreads. An infusion of the fresh leaves is used as a gargle for sore throats, and the oil is used in soaps, lotions, creams, and shampoos.

PRESERVE FOR LATER. Use fresh or dried. The dried leaves do not smell as sharp and clean as the fresh but are still quite tasty. The scent and flavor of sage are strong enough to air-dry, and the attractive, aromatic plants lend a nostalgic ambience to the house. Hang bunches of herbs by their stems in a well-ventilated, shaded, warm place. Drying should take 2 to 5 days, depending on temperature and air circulation. Don't dry too long (the more time they hang, the more flavor they lose), and store in an airtight container.

PART OF PLANT USED	Leaves
CULINARY COMPANIONS	Thyme, savory, meats, cheese, beans
USE TIP	The flavor intensifies with drying. One teaspoon of dried sage equals one tablespoon of chopped fresh sage.

Drying bunches of sage, rosemary, and garlic

Making Herbal Marinades

For the best flavor, grilled foods are often either steeped in a seasoned liquid — marinated — prior to grilling, or they are basted during cooking. At its most basic, a marinade contains only oil and seasonings, so the type and quality of herbs make a big impact on flavor. This combination simply moistens the surface of the food to prevent evaporation of the natural juices during cooking, spreads the flavor of the seasonings over the surface, and prevents the surface from sticking to the grill. With the addition of an acidic liquid, such as vinegar, fruit juice, wine, or soured milk products, the marinade also tenderizes and causes the seasonings to penetrate.

Experiment with different kinds of herbs, oils, and vinegars; there are no hard-and-fast rules, though you may find you enjoy certain herbs better with poultry or fish than with beef, and vice versa.

Red Wine Marinade

Use with beef or lamb.

- ¼ cup olive oil
- 1 cup minced onion
- 2 cloves garlic, minced
- ½ cup garlic red wine vinegar
- ¾ cup dry red wine
- ½ cup water
- ¼ cup tomato paste
- 1 tablespoon fresh rosemary, minced
- 1 bay leaf

1. In a heavy nonreactive skillet, warm the oil over medium heat; add the onion and garlic. Reduce the heat to low and cook until softened, about 5 minutes. Stir in the vinegar and cook until reduced by half.

2. Add the wine, water, tomato paste, rosemary, and bay leaf. Simmer for 5 minutes. Let cool and transfer to a glass or ceramic dish.

MAKES 2 CUPS

Herb-Spice Marinade

Use with chicken or seafood.

1 cup olive oil
¼ cup homemade mixed-herb white wine vinegar (see page 101)
¼ cup lemon juice
1 tablespoon minced fresh cilantro
1 tablespoon minced fresh chives
1 teaspoon ground cumin
1 clove garlic, minced

Combine all the ingredients in a glass or ceramic dish.

MAKES 1½ CUPS

Apple-Sage Marinade

Use with pork.

⅔ cup apple juice
⅓ cup canola or safflower oil
¼ cup homemade sage cider vinegar (see page 101)
2 tablespoons minced fresh sage
1 teaspoon salt

Combine all the ingredients in a glass or ceramic dish.

MAKES 1¼ CUPS

White Wine Marinade

Use with chicken or pork.

⅔ cup dry white wine or vermouth
3 tablespoons olive oil
3 tablespoons homemade mixed-herb or mixed-spice white wine vinegar (see page 101)
¼ cup thinly sliced green onion
¼ cup minced lovage or celery leaves
1 teaspoon minced fresh thyme
1 teaspoon bruised juniper berries (optional)
1 bay leaf
1 clove garlic, minced
¼ teaspoon freshly ground black pepper

Combine all the ingredients in a glass or ceramic dish.

MAKES 1¼ CUPS

Savory

Satureja hortensis (summer savory) and *S. montana* (winter savory)

Winter savory is among the most aromatic of all herbs, with a strong spicy flavor reminiscent of pepper. It is native to the Mediterranean region; the Romans, who used it to flavor many dishes, brought it north to England. Winter savory is a shrubby, compact plant with narrow, dark green foliage. The leaves are evergreen in the southern part of its range, semievergreen in the northern. Summer savory is an annual with slightly longer leaves than winter savory, but it is grown and used in the same way. Summer savory is topped with tiny, pale pink flowers in summer.

Two Types, One Growing Method

Summer and winter savory require the same care when growing, though remember that summer savory is an annual, so it will die after it blooms.

GROW IT. Many people purchase plants from the garden center to get a jump on the season, but savory can also be grown from seeds. Sow indoors in early spring in flats and cover lightly, or direct-sow in late spring. Space or thin the plants to about 1 foot apart. Prevent root rot by providing good drainage.

HARVEST YOUR BOUNTY. Harvest the fresh leaves as needed. Collect leaves for drying just before the flower buds open.

SOIL	Well drained
LIGHT	Full sun
PLANT TYPE	Annual (summer savory); perennial (winter savory)
HARDINESS	Zones 6–9 (winter savory)

OTHER HERBS TO SAVOR

Herbs go in and out of favor with cooks as cooking styles change. It wasn't so long ago that cilantro was practically unheard of, and basil was mostly found dried. Other culinary herbs to consider growing include:

CHERVIL: A delicate herb with hints of anise and parsley. Use as a substitute for tarragon or parsley.

LOVAGE: A hardy herb that tastes like celery combined with parsley. Use instead of celery.

PERILLA: Known as shiso to Japanese cooks, it is popular in Asian pickles and tastes like a cross between cumin, cinnamon, and parsley.

Savor Your Vegetables

Savory is a common ingredient in prepared meats, but it's a friend to vegetables too. In fact, savory is known as the "bean herb" because its flavor goes so well in dried bean dishes.

USES. Winter savory is spicier than summer savory. Infusions of winter savory were once used to relieve the discomfort of indigestion and as a gargle for sore throats. A strong tea made from the fresh leaves was also used as a skin wash to relieve the itch of insect bites. Today, the leaves of savory season prepared meats, such as sausage, vegetable dishes, and stuffings, and they are often blended with butter or soft cheese.

PRESERVE FOR LATER. Dry leaves on screens in a cool, shady place or in the refrigerator. If drying in the refrigerator, do so on paper towel–lined trays, hanging in mesh bags, or in uncovered bowls stirred daily. Drying takes 2 to 7 days. Store in airtight containers. The flavor is also preserved through freezing.

PART OF PLANT USED	Leaves
CULINARY COMPANIONS	Beans, vegetables
USE TIP	Use summer savory fresh in the summer; use winter savory in the winter.

Making Seasoning Blends

Herbal blends are a great way to add flavor to a dish without adding sodium. Some blends can work well on just about anything — eggs, salad, meat, even toast. Others are best for meat, poultry, or seafood. Meat seasonings are versatile. Sprinkle the herb mixture directly on the meat, add it to breadcrumbs for coating before frying or baking, or blend it with oil, vinegar, or soy sauce to make a marinade or basting sauce. Many seafood blends would work nicely in a potato soup or cream-based soup as well.

Herbes de Provence

Herbes de Provence is a blend of dried herbs characteristic of the cooking of southern France. Typically, the blend will contain dried basil, fennel seed, lavender, marjoram, rosemary, sage, summer savory, and thyme. The herb mix is excellent in tomato dishes such as bouillabaisse, and with lamb.

3 tablespoons dried basil
3 tablespoons dried marjoram
3 tablespoons dried thyme
2 tablespoons dried summer savory
1½ teaspoons dried rosemary
½ teaspoon dried lavender flowers
½ teaspoon dried sage
½ teaspoon fennel seeds

Combine all the ingredients and store in a covered jar.

MAKES ABOUT ¾ CUP

All-Purpose Meat Seasoning

Lucinda Lux, of The Secret Garden Herb Shoppe, developed this all-purpose blend for seasoning all kinds of meats and poultry.

3 parts crumbled bay leaf
2 parts rubbed sage
2 parts dried marjoram
1 part dried oregano
1 part dried thyme
1 part dried basil
1 part dried rosemary
1 part dried savory
½ part dried French tarragon

Mix all the ingredients together and store in an airtight glass container. Sprinkle on meat or poultry along with onion and garlic powder before roasting or broiling. Discard bay leaf pieces before eating. Do not consume bay leaves!

All-Purpose Seasoning Blend

Liz Kazio, of The Lavender Garden, developed this all-purpose blend that can be made with or without salt, depending on your preference.

5 tablespoons dried parsley
3 tablespoons dried oregano
2½ tablespoons paprika
2 tablespoons celery seed
2 tablespoons mustard seed
1 tablespoon dried marjoram
1 tablespoon garlic powder
2 teaspoons crushed dried chile
1½ teaspoons dried savory
1 teaspoon dried thyme
1 teaspoon chili powder blend
Salt (optional)

Combine all the herbs and spices and salt to taste, if using, in a blender, spice grinder, or mortar and pestle and finely grind. Store in an airtight container away from heat and light.

MAKES 2⅓ CUPS

Tarragon

Artemisia dracunculus

Tarragon is but one of three hundred species of aromatic herbs belonging to the genus *Artemisia* and collectively called wormwoods. Tarragon has a somewhat bitter but pleasing taste and an ability to produce a warm sensation in the body. The plant has pliant, sometimes woody stems and thin, green, aromatic leaves. The variety *sativa,* or French tarragon, is best used for cooking. Avoid *A. dracunculoides,* or Russian tarragon, for culinary use. It has little taste. Since plants are frequently mislabeled at nurseries, the best way to tell if a plant is French tarragon is to nibble on a leaf. The flavor of citrus and minty pepper should explode in your mouth.

A Little Dragon

Known for having a dragonlike web of tangled roots, tarragon must be divided every few years.

GROW IT. French tarragon is unusual in that it does not seed (Russian tarragon will). Plants should be purchased from commercial nurseries or propagated by dividing established plantings. The name "tarragon" comes from the French word for "little dragon" and refers to the shape of the roots. These roots tend to entangle themselves over the course of a few growing seasons, making division of the plants not simply a method of propagation but also a necessity for the continued welfare of the plants. Container-grown tarragon is a good choice for the winter windowsill garden. In acid soils, add some wood ashes to help keep the pH in the appropriate range.

HARVEST YOUR BOUNTY. To harvest, cut the stems from plants in early summer in the cool of the morning; repeat at the end of the season. Stop harvesting in fall to discourage winter damage.

SOIL	Well drained
LIGHT	Partial to full shade
PLANT TYPE	Perennial
HARDINESS	Zones (4) 5–7

DIVIDING

To divide plants, start in early spring by loosening dirt around the roots. Use a spade to cut through roots to make a division, lifting the cut portion out of the ground with the spade. If your plant is healthy, replace dirt around the remaining roots. Rinse the dirt off the roots of the division and set in a pot of light soil, preferably with added perlite, covering only the roots. Water with care but avoid saturating.

Hungry for More?

Tarragon is known to encourage an appetite, and it's best with eggs, poultry, fish, and vegetables — especially young carrots, green beans, peas, and asparagus.

USES. Tarragon is used to stimulate the appetite and to flavor mustards, soups, poultry, eggs, dressings, and stuffing. For the bath, it is added to soaps, shampoos, lotions, and even toothpaste.

PRESERVE FOR LATER. Dry the leaves in the microwave for 1 to 3 minutes (check every minute — they are done when they are dry to the touch but haven't lost any color) or in an uncovered bowl in the refrigerator (stirring daily). You can also freeze for later use and then store them in an airtight container. Leaves prepared by traditional drying methods often lose a good measure of their flavor.

PART OF PLANT USED	Leaves
CULINARY COMPANIONS	Chervil, chives, parsley
USE TIP	Don't combine tarragon with other resinous herbs, such as rosemary or sage.

Tarragon leaves
sautéed with shrimp

Making Mustards

Liven up your mustard by adding fresh herbs, vinegar, and honey or brown sugar. Experiment with different vinegars and herbs, using either a single herb or a mixture, matching the vinegar to the fresh herbs or using complementary ones. Some of the herbs to try with mustards include the basils, burnet, celery seed, chervil, chilies, chives, cilantro leaves or seeds, dill leaves or seeds, fennel leaves or seeds, garlic chives, horseradish, parsley, rosemary, tarragon, and the thymes. Be sure to try fruit vinegars, too, matching the vinegar and fruit juice. Consider raspberry and other bramble fruits, blueberry, and cranberry.

Basic Mustard

Think of this as your blueprint for a basic herbal mustard. Experiment and let your taste buds run wild!

- ½ cup light or dark mustard seeds
- ¼ cup dry English mustard
- ¾ cup herb or other flavored vinegar
- ⅔ cup water, wine, beer, or fruit juice
- ¼ cup fresh minced herbs, or 2 tablespoons ground herb seeds
- 2 tablespoons honey or 3 tablespoons white or packed brown sugar
- 1 teaspoon salt

1. Combine mustard seeds, dry mustard, vinegar, and other liquid in a medium nonreactive bowl. Let sit for 4 hours, uncovered, stirring occasionally.

2. Transfer to a blender or food processor. Process to the desired texture, from slightly coarse to creamy.

3. Pour into the top of a double boiler over simmering water. Stir in the remaining ingredients. Cook for 10 minutes, or until thickened, stirring often. The mustard will be thicker when cooled. Pour into sterilized jars, cap tightly, and store in the refrigerator. Wait several days before using to allow the flavors to blend.

MAKES 2 CUPS

Tarragon Mustard

This mustard is only available if you make it. It tastes especially good on a chicken sandwich.

- 3 tablespoons dry mustard
- 2 tablespoons light or dark mustard seeds
- ½ teaspoon salt
- 1 pinch ground turmeric (optional — it's mostly for color)
- ⅔ cup less 1 tablespoon boiling water
- ¼ cup homemade tarragon white wine vinegar (see page 101)
- ¼ cup white wine

1. Put the dry mustard, mustard seeds, salt, and turmeric (if you're using it) into a small saucepan. Stir in the boiling water. Let sit for 45 minutes.

2. Add the tarragon vinegar and white wine. Pour the contents of the pan into a food processor and run the machine until the mixture is smooth. (It's all right for it to be a little lumpy, though, because of the mustard seeds.)

3. Return to the saucepan. Cook over very low heat, stirring and scraping, until the mustard has thickened slightly.

4. Remove to a sterilized jar. Cover when cool, then keep under refrigeration.

MAKES ABOUT 1 CUP

Sherry-Thyme Mustard

Try this on a meatloaf sandwich, or anything that contains onion or garlic.

- ½ cup light or dark mustard seeds
- 2 tablespoons dry English mustard
- ½ cup dry sherry
- ½ cup homemade thyme sherry vinegar (see page 101)
- 2 tablespoons honey
- 2 tablespoons minced fresh thyme
- 2 teaspoons salt

1. Combine the mustard seeds, dry mustard, sherry, and vinegar in a small nonreactive bowl. Let sit for 4 hours, uncovered, stirring occasionally.

2. Transfer to a blender or food processor. Process to the desired texture, from slightly coarse to creamy.

3. Pour into the top of a double boiler over simmering water. Stir in the remaining ingredients. Cook for 10 minutes, or until thickened, stirring often. The mustard will be thicker when cooled.

4. Pour into sterilized jars, cap tightly, and store in the refrigerator. Wait several days before using to allow the flavors to blend.

MAKES 1½ CUPS

Thyme

Thymus spp.

The most popular thymes have small, mouse-ear leaves that are strongly aromatic. The scent of common thyme is so pungently spicy that it seems to lend acuity to the senses; other thymes mimic the aromas of lemon, caraway, and nutmeg. Many thymes are low-growing or creeping plants that are at home in the herb garden, in crevices, or cascading over walls and rock gardens. Thyme is a hardy perennial and will grow in most climates, though it does best in well-drained soils. Prune it back in the spring by about a third to keep it vigorous and avoid woodiness. Prune again after flowering to encourage a second flowering.

A Woody, Good Grower

Many varieties of thyme grow out rather than up, creating a pungent carpet in your garden. Some people like to plant it between stones on a pathway, or even just on their lawn.

GROW IT. Sow seeds indoors in flats, keeping the soil just above room temperature; they can also be direct-sown in late spring. Transplant or thin the plants to 1 foot apart. As the plants become established and woody, they will benefit from being divided every 3 to 5 years. If leaf production declines, replace plants rather than divide them. Mulch in late fall with leaves, pine needles, or straw.

HARVEST YOUR BOUNTY. Harvest the leaves anytime, but for maximum flavor, harvest sprigs just before bloom. Stop harvesting in late summer to discourage winter damage.

SOIL	Well drained
LIGHT	Full sun to partial shade
PLANT TYPE	Perennial
HARDINESS	Zones 5–9

THE LANGUAGE OF HERBS

Since the Middle Ages, flowers and herbs have been associated with emotions, and scenting a dish or a handkerchief with a certain herb would communicate a feeling to the recipient. Here are some common herbs and their meanings.

DILL: Lust

GARLIC: Courage, strength

LAVENDER: Love, devotion

MARJORAM: Joy, happiness

MINT: Virtue

PARSLEY: Useful knowledge

ROSEMARY: Remembrance

SAGE: Wisdom

Makes Nice with Other Spice!

Most herbs play well with others, but this is especially true for thyme. Many different types of dishes and herbs will benefit from its company.

USES. Thyme has been used since ancient times to treat a number of complaints, including anxiety. Today warm infusions are said to alleviate congestion, relieve the pain of headaches, and ease stomach complaints. A blend of sage, lavender, and thyme eases coughs. As a culinary herb, thyme has a strong but pliant taste that both supports and accents the flavor of many dishes. The fresh or dried leaves can be added to sauces, stews, meats, fish, poultry, eggs, dressings, and stuffings. Thyme also mixes well with other seasonings, such as garlic and lemon. The delicate flowers of thyme attract honeybees.

PRESERVE FOR LATER. Dry leaves in the refrigerator for best results: Gently wash sprigs with cool water, and allow to air-dry. Place in the refrigerator on paper towel–lined trays, hanging in mesh bags, or in uncovered bowls (stir daily). Herbs will take 2 to 7 days to dry. Store in airtight containers. The flavor of thyme is also preserved through freezing.

PART OF PLANT USED	Leaves
CULINARY COMPANIONS	Garlic, lemon, onion
USE TIP	Dry in refrigerator

Making Herbal Oils

Herb-flavored oils are another way to add the essence of your herbs to cooking. Use a light oil (such as olive, safflower, or sunflower) and a strongly flavored herb, such as basil, bay, oregano, rosemary, or thyme.

1. Clean the fresh herb and allow it to dry thoroughly (this is extremely important, as wet herbs will cause spoilage).

2. Fill a sterilized bottle or jar one-quarter to one-third of the way full with herbs, and fill the rest with oil. Be sure that all the herbs are submersed in oil.

3. Cap the bottle and let stand at room temperature, out of direct sunlight, for 10 to 14 days.

4. Strain the oil through a clean, dry cotton cloth, and discard the herb.

5. Store the oil out of direct light and extreme heat or in the refrigerator. Use within 2 months to avoid spoilage (bad oil will have a very pungent smell).

You will find plenty of uses for herbal oils once you have some in the cupboard. Start with salad dressings, using the herbal oil in your favorite vinaigrette (see page 91). Try drizzling it on a platter of sliced tomatoes. A light drizzle of herbal oil on grilled chicken breasts or fish adds both flavor and needed moisture. Drizzle it on steamed vegetables as a heart-healthy (and delicious) alternative to butter. You can also serve a shallow bowl of herbed oil along with crusty bread.

When roasting or grilling vegetables, it is a good idea to coat the veggies with oil to encourage browning and to prevent the vegetables from drying out. Using herbal oils adds a whole new flavor dimension.

HERBS AT A GLANCE

Perennial Herbs	SOIL	LIGHT	PLANTING DISTANCE	FULL HEIGHT	PART TO HARVEST
ANISE HYSSOP	Fertile, well drained	○ ◐	12 in.	3 ft.	Leaves, flowers
BAY	Well drained, ordinary	○ ◐	—	20 ft.	Leaves
BEE BALM	Ordinary, moist	○ ◐	18 in.	3 ft.	Stems, leaves, flowers
CATNIP	Sandy, dry	○ ◐	18 in.	3 ft.	Stems, leaves
CHIVES	Rich	○	8 in.	8–12 in.	Stems, leaves, flowers
FENNEL	Well limed	○	18 in.	5 ft.	Stems, leaves, seeds
GARLIC	Well drained, rich	○	6 in.	1 ft.	Bulb
HYSSOP	Well drained, light	○ ◐	12 in.	1½ ft.	Stems, leaves, flowers
LAVENDER	Well drained, light	○	36 in.	2½ ft.	Stems, leaves, flowers
LEMON BALM	Well drained, sandy	○ ◐	18 in.	4 ft.	Stems, leaves
LEMON VERBENA	Rich, evenly moist	○	24–36 in.	Up to 8 ft.	Stems, leaves
MARJORAM	Rich, light	○	12 in.	9–12 in.	Stems, leaves
MINTS, ALL	Rich, well drained	○ ◐	18 in.	3 ft.	Stems, leaves
OREGANO	Well drained	○	18 in.	1½ ft.	Stems, leaves
ROSEMARY	Well drained, light	○	36 in.	4–5 ft.	Stems, leaves
SAGE	Sandy, limed, well drained	○ ◐	24 in.	1½ ft.	Stems, leaves
SAVORY, WINTER	Poor, well drained	○	12 in.	8 in.	Stems, leaves
TARRAGON	Well drained, light	◐ ●	12 in.	2 ft.	Stems, leaves
THYME	Sandy, well drained	○ ◐	12 in.	10 in.	Stems, leaves

Annual and Biennial Herbs	SOIL	LIGHT	PLANTING DISTANCE	FULL HEIGHT	PART TO HARVEST
BASIL	Rich	○	12 in.	1½ ft.	Seeds, stems, leaves, flowers
BORAGE	Well drained, ordinary	○ ◐	18 in.	3 ft.	Leaves, flowers
CALENDULA	Well drained, light, sandy	○	12 in.	2 ft.	Flowers
CARAWAY	Ordinary	○	8 in.	2 ft.	Seeds, leaves, roots
CILANTRO & CORIANDER	Ordinary	○	4 in.	2–3 ft.	Leaves, seeds
DILL	Light, sandy	○	10 in.	3 ft.	Leaves, seeds
PARSLEY	Rich	○ ◐	8 in.	8–12 in.	Stems, leaves
SAVORY, SUMMER	Light, rich	○	8 in.	1½ ft.	Stems, leaves

LIGHT ○ Full Sun ◐ Part Shade ● Full Shade

VEGETABLE COMPANIONS	USE HERB FOR
	Flavoring salads, sauces, teas
	Flavoring sauces, soups, stews
	Salads (flowers); teas (leaves)
	Flavoring salads, sauces, stews, teas
Carrots, tomatoes	Flavoring cheeses, salads, soups, stews
	Flavoring breads, fish, salads, sausages, teas
Beets, broccoli, onions, tomatoes	Flavoring wide variety of foods
Cabbage family	Flavoring salads, soups, stews, teas
	Beverage garnish, desserts, jellies, oils, tea, wines
Swiss chard	Salads, teas, vinegars
	Flavoring salads, stuffings, teas
	Flavoring salads, meats, teas, vegetables
Beans, broccoli	Flavoring beverages, desserts, jellies
	Flavoring pasta, pizza sauce, stews, teas
Broccoli, cabbage family, carrots	Flavoring meat dishes, sauces, soups, stews, teas
Broccoli, cabbage family, carrots	Seasoning cheeses, poultry, sausage, teas
Beans	Flavoring eggs, meats, vegetables
	Flavoring mustards, poultry, soups
Cabbage family	Seasoning fish, meats, soups, stuffings

VEGETABLE COMPANIONS	USE HERB FOR
Garlic, onion, peppers, tomatoes	Flavoring meats, stuffings, tomato-based sauces, vegetables
Squash, tomatoes	Cucumber-flavored leaves and flowers good in salads, teas
Asparagus	Flower petal used in bread, butter, cheese spreads, rice dishes, soups, stews
Peas	Seeds flavor breads, cheeses, meats; leaves flavor salads
	Confections (seeds); salads (leaves); oils
Broccoli, cabbage, cucumbers, tomatoes,	Flavoring pickles, salads, sauces, soups
Asparagus, celery, peas, tomatoes,	Flavoring salads, sauces, soups, stews
Bush beans, green beans, pole beans	Flavoring eggs, meats, string beans

Index

Italicized page references indicate line art and photographs.
Bold page references indicate charts and tables.

Other Storey Titles You Will Enjoy

The Gardener's A–Z Guide to Growing Organic Food,
by Tanya L. K. Denckla.
An invaluable resource for growing, harvesting, and storing 765 varieties
of vegetables, fruits, herbs, and nuts.
496 pages. Paper. ISBN 978-1-58017-370-4.

The Herb Gardener, **by Susan McClure.**
Herb gardening basics for every season, indoors and out.
240 pages. Paper. ISBN 978-0-88266-873-4.

Starter Vegetable Gardens, **by Barbara Pleasant.**
A great resource for beginning vegetable gardeners: 24 no-fail plans for
small organic gardens.
192 pages. Paper. ISBN 978-1-60432-529-2.

The Vegetable Gardener's Bible, 2nd edition, **by Edward C. Smith.**
The 10th Anniversary Edition of the vegetable gardening classic, with
expanded coverage of additional vegetables, fruits, and herbs.
352 pages. Paper. ISBN 978-1-60342-475-2.

The Veggie Gardener's Answer Book, **by Barbara W. Ellis.**
Insider's tips and tricks, practical advice, and organic wisdom for
vegetable growers everywhere.
432 pages. Paper. ISBN 978-1-60342-024-2.

These and other books from Storey Publishing are available
wherever quality books are sold or by calling 1-800-441-5700.
Visit us at *www.storey.com.*